THE EVAL
of
SELF TEST

THE EVALUATION of SELF TEST

Your Answers Can Transform
Your Self and Your Life

Created by

ANTHONY EUGENE VANN

for my Mom

Thank you for your love, support, and guidance.

Acknowledgements

I would like to thank everyone that helped me during my journey to complete this creative work.

I could not have completed it without the full support of my wife Sharon, my daughter, Danielle, my son, Marcel and my brother Kevin. In addition, a special thank you to my sisters Juanita and Ramona for reviewing the work and providing valuable feedback.

I would like to express my gratitude as well to the person that edited my work and provided encouraging feedback that kept me motivated until final publishing. Thank you so much, Aya Summers, for the time and effort you provided to help me.

And finally, I must give a special thank you to my Pastor, Dr. Reginald Garmon, whose sermons always provided the words of encouragement I needed to remain faithful in my efforts to achieve my goal of completing this work. I dreamed of writing this book many years ago and he continually reminded me that dreams are "Divinely Revealed Events Awaiting Manifestation." Thank you Pastor Garmon. My dream has manifested.

> *"Seek to understand;*
> *To understand differences in thought*
> *To bring clarity and peace*
> *Into all of your relationships with other people*
> *and in all of your life situations."*
>
> Anthony E. Vann

Contents

Introduction 1

The Need for Self Evaluation 4

Knowing Your Purpose 20

Understanding Your Life Situations Part One 49

Understanding Your Life Situations Part Two 82

Understanding the Importance of Goals 104

Living a Balanced Life 136

The Review 186

Period of Reflection 192

Introduction

Congratulations! You have taken the first step required for the process of change to begin. By opening this book and reading these pages, you have unleashed the seeds of knowledge that will hopefully grow and flourish in your mind in the near future.

The seeds of knowledge contained in the following pages will stimulate your imagination. They will engage the creative thinking process within you that is necessary to generate new ideas and new ways of being, existing, and thinking about your Self and the life you are living.

The Evaluation of Self Test (TEST) contains thought-provoking questions that will help you to determine what has led you to your current state of being and assist you in determining what you want for your Self in the days ahead.

Please keep in mind that it is my hope that you can apply all of the concepts and ideas presented to you but not everything within these pages may currently apply to you; it may not be relevant for you to use each and every solution provided.

However, it is my goal to provide you with a tool for change. I will have achieved that goal if you are able to use at least one idea from this book to make a positive change in your Self and your life.

The ideas within these pages can be used to change any aspect of your Self and your life such as your career or professional life, your family and personal relationships,

The Evaluation of Self Test

your health and finances, as well as personal traits such as patience, discipline, reliability, confidence, initiative, and many more. But it is all up to you.

You can choose to do one of two things:

1. Read this book and not change anything about your Self or the life you are living and thus continue to exist in the same manner and create the same type of situations you are experiencing now.
2. You can read this book, complete a thorough evaluation of your Self and the situations you have created, decide everything is good or decide that a change is required. If change is required, use the ideas and tools provided to create a plan of action and then act.

What will you choose?

But before we go any further there is a prerequisite required in order to prepare you for the information you are about to read. The prerequisite is that each time you begin reading any part of the TEST, perform the following:

1. Remove as many distractions as possible from around you. Ensure your surroundings are peaceful.
2. Relax your mind and body by first putting a big smile on your face and taking five to ten deep, calming breaths. Do this now.
3. Lastly, open your mind! Say to your Self either aloud or in your head something that prepares your mind to receive the information you are about to

Introduction

read. You can use a favorite prayer or simply state the following as you are smiling and breathing deeply: "I am ready to receive these seeds of knowledge with an open mind, an open heart, and without judgment."

Once you have relaxed your mind and body, you may begin reading. Follow this prerequisite each time you open the book to read. If you find your Self starting without completing the prerequisite, ask your Self, "Why am I rushing? What's the hurry?"

Remember, if you can't take the five minutes or less to complete the prerequisite, will you ever take the time to allow the seeds of knowledge provided in each chapter to grow in your mind in order to change your life?

And one last thing: unless you borrowed this book from someone, this is your book. So make it your book. Write in it, underline words and highlight areas that are significant to you. Make notes on the outer edges of the text.

Identify any areas where a quote can be used to create an affirmation. Use different color ink or pencil to help certain topics stand out. Do whatever you need to identify key areas for you to review during a quick read or to help you grasp the concept that was being presented.

You are now ready to read The Evaluation of Self Test.

Chapter One

The Need for Self Evaluation

The Process of Evaluation

Like most seventeen-year-olds, I didn't't have a clue about what I really wanted after I graduated from high school. But there was one thing I did know; I needed a job to earn some money. I was also in need of some serious direction and guidance for my life ahead.

As luck would have it, I was provided with exactly what I needed from my first job. It was at this first job that I was introduced to the Process of Evaluation.

When I was first hired, I never would have thought that the Process of Evaluation would be the key to the success I enjoy today. This Process of Evaluation provided me with the guidance and direction I needed for growth in my career and personal life for twenty one years.

This Process of Evaluation, which I profited from in so many ways, inspired me to write this book, The Evaluation of Self Test (TEST).

Evaluations

At some point in your life, you may have been evaluated by someone to let you know how well or how poorly you performed on a given assignment or job. It may have been a written evaluation, verbal, or a combination of

The Need for Self Evaluation

both. Just about every corporation or business conducts evaluations, reviews, or performance appraisals on their employees similar to the kind my first employer used with me.

These evaluations are used to determine eligibility for jobs, advancement, bonuses and salary increases. They are also used to evaluate your performance on the job; your value to the company.

Additionally, you may discuss any future goals you may have that will be of benefit to the company as well as the company's goals and the role you will play to meet them.

These evaluations especially allow the employer, usually an immediate supervisor or manager, an opportunity to conduct a face-to-face session with the employee to let them know exactly what they think of them and their job performance. Sometimes the evaluation matches how the employee feels they have performed but more often than not, the employee feels they have performed better than their employer's appraisal.

These types of evaluations are usually forced upon the employee as a requirement of employment. They are conducted by other people, using standards and measures they have developed. And while I benefited greatly from the evaluations provided by my employer, I never had or knew of anything else I could use to evaluate my Self with.

So the question is: What tool are you using to evaluate your Self? How do you evaluate your current state of being? What standards do you use to determine your performance at work, at home, in your personal relationships or in managing your money?

The Evaluation of Self Test

What do you use to evaluate your health or level of education? To evaluate your ability to resolve issues related to the most important matters in your life?

Are you setting goals to improve your Self in any of these areas? Are you using anything to provoke new thoughts and ideas regarding your personal life or future? Are you currently using anything to conduct periodic evaluations on your Self to determine if you are taking responsibility for your life and the situations you are creating?

If not, the TEST is exactly what you need. And if the answer is yes, the TEST can serve as an additional tool, a helpful option that can be used to validate and complement what you are already using. The Process of Evaluation contained in this book is for your use, not your employer.

The TEST is a tool for you to evaluate your Self and the lifestyle you are living. It will provoke the thoughts and ideas that are necessary for you to understand your Self better and create a lifestyle of your own choosing; to create a life filled with peace, happiness, and success in whatever it is you choose to pursue.

Each chapter will challenge you to examine, measure, analyze, explore and evaluate your Self by one, answering numerous questions, two, completing a quiz at the end of each chapter, and three, completing several exercises designed to strengthen your understanding of the concepts being provided.

These three requirements will help you identify areas of your thinking and behavior that may require a change. And you will discover that the areas where change will most

The Need for Self Evaluation

commonly be required will be in your beliefs, environment, actions, conditioning, or habits.

The TEST provides you with an opportunity to look in the mirror and see the real you; the you that is hidden from everyone else because it resides within you. The evaluations conducted on you by corporations, businesses, and other people document what they feel about you — their perception of you.

And while these evaluations serve an important function, only you can perform an honest and true evaluation of your Self.

'Self' has been purposefully separated from 'yourself' because it is a separate entity within you; it is your inner being, your consciousness, that thinking part of you or the voice in your head. This is the part of you that will undergo the evaluation. The you that nobody else knows or sees; the you that's reading this book. Because this is where real change has to begin — within your Self.

The Test

The TEST is also an actual test. It is a test to see if you are willing to do the work that is necessary to complete a thorough evaluation of your Self as well as the situations you have created in your life. You will easily pass this test if you answer all of the questions, complete all of the quizzes, and complete all of the exercises presented to you.

And yes, I hear you…not another test! Those are the words that come to mind anytime I'm asked to answer questions for a test, exam, or evaluation. But I have come

The Evaluation of Self Test

to realize that tests serve a very important purpose. Tests evaluate something to see where it stands today; not tomorrow, now, at this moment in time. Tomorrow's results could be different.

Tests give us a point of reference, a standard that we can use to determine if some type of correction or change is needed. And let's face it, you never know the truth about your Self, your level of knowledge, how you respond under pressure and so many other things until you put your Self to the test, until you look in the mirror and evaluate your Self as no one else can. This book, the TEST, provides you with that very thing.

You will evaluate your Self by using four Personal Development Solutions. These will be covered in greater detail shortly. Each Personal Development Solution contains information that is used for your Self-evaluation as well as evaluating the situations you have created. This is where the work must be completed in order to pass the test.

You will do exceptionally well in completing a thorough evaluation of your Self as well as pass the test if you answer all of the questions, complete all exercises, and complete each quiz contained in the Personal Development Solutions. Again, this is for your benefit. If you are not ready to put the time in to complete the work, the Personal Development Solutions will be of no benefit to you and you will not pass the test.

But more importantly, you will miss out on the opportunity to bring clarity into your thinking regarding your Self and the situations in which you are participating.

Reading The Evaluation of Self Test is easy. Completing the work and changing your Self and the

The Need for Self Evaluation

situations you are creating will be the hardest part of the process. It can be difficult for some people to answer questions about how they think and feel or assess their strengths and weaknesses. Changing any aspect of your thoughts, emotions, and behavior can be a constant struggle.

Keep this in mind as you read through the book: it's not about seeking perfection. Your goal should be to bring order into each area of your life if and where it does not already exist. This should ultimately bring more happiness and peace into your life.

Your Self-evaluation will be like the Portrait of Dorian Gray. In the movie of the same title, Dorian's portrait reflects the pain of his life on his face, in monstrous detail. The results of your Self-evaluation, your test results, may paint an unflattering picture of you and the life you are living.

It is my hope that it will paint a pretty picture or one that only needs a little touch-up. But there will not be a picture if you don't provide honest answers during the Self-evaluation process.

Personal Development

One of the goals of this book is to help you develop into the person you want to become while living a lifestyle that brings you peace, happiness, and success in whatever you choose to undertake. This goal will be achieved when you complete your Self-evaluation and take the action that is necessary for you to improve in any area of your life you feel is lacking or deficient.

The Evaluation of Self Test

But in order for this to occur and this Self-evaluation to be a success, a personal choice has to be made by you to complete it. Going into this halfheartedly will not be of benefit to you so make your decision now. No one is forcing this on you so the choice is yours.

But by continuing to read this book, you will have decided to change something about your Self. You will have decided to develop into the kind of person that takes control of their thoughts, actions, and behavior.

Again, please don't fool your Self into thinking this will be easy. A real, long term commitment of your time and energy is required here. You must plant the seeds of knowledge provided in the form of Personal Development Solutions into your thoughts so they can grow and become a part of your mindset, your lifestyle, and your day to day living.

True change has to occur in the mind first— in your "Self". You can change a hundred things outside of your Self and not see or feel like any real change has occurred in your life. Hundreds if not thousands of people lose weight from dieting and exercise every year. But a large percentage of them still think and view themselves as being overweight.

They lost the weight but did not lose the overweight thought or image they had within their Self. This is one of the many reasons people gain the weight back. But by changing what's inside of you first, your Self, your thoughts and images (internally), it will be much easier to change anything outside of your Self (externally). This is the type of change that can last a lifetime.

The Need for Self Evaluation

Personal Development Solutions

The Personal Development Solutions provided in the coming chapters is the start of change, true change. They will take you on a journey through your Self. They are the tools by which you will evaluate your Self. They will help you evaluate your thoughts and feelings which have been dictating your actions. With this knowledge in hand, you can then evaluate your actions which have over time, determined your behavior.

Once you can clearly see what your behavior has been, you will be in a better position to evaluate your attitude towards life, your life situations, and the world around you like you have never seen it before.

The success of your Self-evaluation and your future development will depend greatly on your ability to apply the knowledge you gain from the Personal Development Solutions to your internal Self and the external situations you are involved in.

There are four Personal Development Solutions presented. They are:

1. Knowing Your Purpose
2. Understanding Your Life Situation
3. Understanding the Importance of Setting Goals
4. Living a Balanced Life

Each Solution provides you with valuable thought-provoking information to make you more aware of your current situation and what is necessary to change any aspect of it. As I mentioned earlier, each chapter has a quiz to complete at the end.

The Evaluation of Self Test

You must answer all of the questions on each quiz to ensure you have absorbed the information. These quizzes will also help stimulate the creative ideas that are necessary for you to make important decisions about your Self and your life so that you can start planning your future.

The following is a brief description of each Personal Development Solution that you will evaluate your Self with.

Knowing Your Purpose

We start your evaluation by determining if you know what your purpose is. You will decide what the purpose of your existence is as a creative being. This will establish what the focus of your internal state of being, your Self, is or will be.

You must create a purpose statement before continuing to the next Personal Development Solution. Everything you do after creating this statement will be focused on helping you to achieve it.

Your purpose will be your starting point, or rather, your point of reference from where the many choices and decisions you will need to make will emanate from as you move forward through your Self-evaluation. All of your thoughts and actions must be in agreement with the purpose you choose for your Self.

The Need for Self Evaluation

Understanding Your Life Situation

The next solution is Understanding Your Life Situation. Your life situation is the result of the many choices and decisions you have made in the past and what you think about them as a whole. It includes all the situations you have created or are involved in, such as your job situation, your health situation, your financial situation, your marital situation, or the situation with your coworker, neighbor, or friend, etc.

It is basically everything you might be thinking about if you are not focused on what is happening in the present moment.

You will evaluate the many situations you are currently involved in and determine which ones are problem-free, need improvement and which, if any, are continually problematic. You will also evaluate your beliefs, environment, actions, conditioned responses, and habits related to the situations in your life.

You will then create a philosophy that will establish a plan of action by which you act and behave based on your findings and your unique life situation.

Your plan of action will establish the principles by which you use the creative force within you to change any situation that needs improvement, is continually problematic, or is not in alignment with your purpose. Your philosophy will also provide the direction and guidance you need to create new situations that are in alignment with your purpose as you move forward.

A complete understanding of the situations you are currently involved in is one of the most important factors in your evaluation. Your current life situation and your thoughts and feelings about it will determine if or where a need for change exists.

Understanding the Importance of Setting Goals

This Personal Development Solution will determine if you understand the importance of setting goals. You will evaluate if you know what goals are, how to create them, and what their importance is in your personal development and the process of change.

You will also learn how to create a Measurable Action Plan (MAP). It will serve as your written plan of action to achieve your goals. The MAP will list all of the goals you decide upon to change your Self and your life situations. Your MAP will always be available as needed to guide you during those periods when you lose your way or forget what you are trying to achieve and the reason why.

Living a Balanced Life

And finally, the last solution is, Living a Balanced Life. In this chapter, we will provide our definition of what being in a perfect state of balance is. You will evaluate if you are living a balanced life based on the definition provided. We will also discuss the Five Points on Balance. They are the means by which you can achieve our defined state of balance.

These points focus on what happens inside of you; in your thoughts, in your body's reaction to these thoughts by way of your feelings and emotions, and finally the impact

The Need for Self Evaluation

that these thoughts, feelings, and emotions have on your life situations.

One of the most important of these points is Self-Induced Obstacles. As you begin to change and develop into the person you want to be, Self-Induced Obstacles will begin to surface. We will review these and others and provide ideas on how to remove or reduce their impact on your Self, and your life so that you can live in, or close to, a perfect state of balance.

Evaluation Points

These are your four Personal Development Solutions. They serve as your evaluation tool and your test. Each solution contains evaluation points for you to examine, measure, analyze, explore and evaluate your Self by, one, answering numerous questions, two, completing a quiz at the end of each chapter and three, completing several exercises designed to strengthen your understanding of the concepts being provided.

These solutions will help you begin the process of change that leads to your development into the person you desire to be, living a lifestyle of your choosing. Remember to be patient with your Self and take your time as you read through each chapter. You will complete a thorough evaluation of your Self and your life situation by doing the following:

1. Consider every question that is asked in the Personal Development Solutions, including quizzes, an evaluation point.

The Evaluation of Self Test

2. Pause for a moment or two to assess how each question may relate to you mentally (thoughts), physically, emotionally, or spiritually (feelings).
3. Give extra time and consideration to questions or areas that are identified as important evaluation points.
4. The completion of every exercise should be considered an evaluation point.

These are the procedures you should follow to complete your evaluation. This is where the work must be done. This is where you discover if or where change is needed. And this is what will determine if you will pass the test.

If you find your Self reading through the pages without reflecting for a moment or two on a question you were asked or skipping exercises and leaving answers to quiz questions blank, you are wasting your time. Your evaluation will be incomplete. At this point, you should stop, put the book down and begin again when you feel you are ready to do the work.

Jim Rohn, the great motivational speaker said, "Work harder on your Self than you do on your job." If you work hard at completing this evaluation, just as you would an assignment at your job, you will build an understanding of your Self that will propel you to heights you never thought you could reach. You will reap all of the benefits and rewards in the same manner as I did from the evaluations performed on me by my first employer.

So it is my hope that you are ready, willing, and able to complete your evaluation and in the end, pass the test. But

The Need for Self Evaluation

before we begin, there is one more thing you must be ready to do.

Take Responsibility and Ownership For Your Life

As I said earlier, true change occurs in the mind first. Accepting the truth about what is occurring in your life and taking full responsibility and ownership in changing whatever it is that you are tired of tolerating, is the beginning of a change of mind. Until you take full responsibility for what has occurred or is occurring within your Self and your life, true change cannot happen.

One of the first things Alcoholics Anonymous requires participants to do is to accept they are alcoholics by saying, "Hello, my name is Jim and I'm an alcoholic." You must take responsibility for the situations you have created by saying to your Self, "My name is Jim and I made the choices and decisions that have led me to my current state of being and I either created or chose to participate in the situations I am involved in and I am the only one that can change them."

Don't place the blame anywhere but on your own shoulders. Once you take full ownership of all of the situations you have created, true change can begin.

You will, of course, need the assistance of other people on this life-changing journey. You may not succeed without the help of family, friends, business partners, co-workers, or anyone else that is a part of your life. It is possible to succeed without the help of others but your journey to success will take much longer. The people that assist you will serve as your support group; they will be

The Evaluation of Self Test

your team. Ask them for their opinion or advice when needed.

I believe we are all here to help one another in some form or fashion. So don't be shy about asking for help when another opinion or perspective is needed. You may not like what they have to say but it's probably something you need to hear.

But even with this team effort, you still have to be the leader, the quarterback of the team; you have to be the pilot, not the co-pilot, you have to be the driver of the car, not the passenger. Remember, your progression to success is, again, your ultimate responsibility. You will reap the benefits of success and learn the most from any setbacks or "perceived" failure.

Unfortunately, the word "failure" instills negative thoughts and attitudes. If at any time you feel you have failed at changing something, remember that you haven't failed: You simply learned how something was not supposed to be done. You can never "fail" if you learned something as a result of not accomplishing a task or goal.

Whenever you "fail" at something you must, "Find An Interesting Lesson" in whatever you "failed" at doing. By doing this, the lesson you learned from the "failure" can be applied to your next attempt until you succeed.

There isn't a sports athlete that makes every free throw, catches every pass, or wins every race. But with a minor adjustment here or there, they soon arrive in the winner's circle or hold the champions trophy. It may even take years to find the right combination of choices, decisions, and actions before you succeed. But it has been proven time and time again that the repetition of the right combination

The Need for Self Evaluation

of choices, decisions, and actions eventually leads to success.

So let's begin your evaluation and journey through your Self. All you need is a pen and a notebook or a journal to keep track of all your answers to the many questions you will be asked during your evaluation. Or for those who prefer, grab your laptop or tablet. And keep a mirror handy so you can keep an eye on the ever changing Portrait of

_____.
Your Name

Relax.

Smile.

Complete the prerequisite before continuing to the next chapter.

Chapter Two

Knowing Your Purpose

"When you are inspired by some great purpose, some extraordinary project, all your thoughts break their bonds. Your mind transcends limitations, your consciousness expands in every direction and you find your Self in a new, great wonderful world. Dormant forces, faculties and talents become alive and you discover your Self to be a greater person by far than you ever dreamed your Self to be." Pantanjali

What is your Purpose?

Let's face it, life is about repetition — repetition of thoughts, emotions, and activities. When things are going great, it's easy to be happy with your Self and your life. But what do you do when the repetition of your daily routine and everyone and everything in it becomes a source of boredom? What do you focus on when you begin to feel a bit more anxiety, depression, doubt, or fear regarding the situations in your life?

What do you place the focus of your attention on when your thoughts continually dwell on the negative instead of the positive aspects of your Self and all of the situations you exist in?

You could answer these questions in many ways. But for our purpose here, there is only one. And that is: Place the focus of your attention on the purpose you have established for your Self. Your Self as the peaceful,

Knowing Your Purpose

creative being you naturally are. A purpose that allows the peace and stillness that dwells within you to remain in a stable, balanced state regardless of the situations you may experience and on living a lifestyle that allows you to achieve that purpose daily. Because if you were actually experiencing any of the situations listed above, you would have to change something.

You would have to change your Self. You would have to change the discontented, unsettled state of being you exist in.

This chapter asks the question, "What is your purpose? More specifically, what purpose have you established for your internal state of being — your Self?" Your Self which in its essence is pure existence. Most people can't answer this question.

Your ability to answer this question is important because your lifestyle or rather your philosophy for living a purposeful life will flow from this central idea, this focused state of mind. Your philosophy, which we will discuss in detail in the next chapter, will establish the principles by which you act and behave while you exist and live with purpose.

Your principles will establish the plan of action by which you change any situation in your life that is not in alignment with your purpose. If the situations you are creating or are currently involved in are not a true reflection of what you want, you will be able to easily identify the areas where change is needed. And if they are, you can work on ways to improve or enhance them.

So, can you answer the question: What is your purpose? What purpose have you established for your

The Evaluation of Self Test

internal state of being? For your Self? If your answer is yes, write your purpose down in your notebook and continue to read along to evaluate your answer against the one provided.

But before we continue, the following exercise will help you understand what I am referring to when I describe your "Self" as pure existence. It will also teach you how to control your mind. It will teach you how to control the random and repetitive flow of thoughts that can often consume and overwhelm you and create stress, anxiety, and other negative states.

It does this by focusing your attention and your awareness on your breathing or by your listening to the rhythm of your body as you breathe. It's not about thinking. It's about, feeling, sensing, experiencing, being aware, being attentive to your breath as you float, drift in and out of different states of being and flowing with what is here, in this moment. You're just existing. Read the following information thoroughly first, and then perform the exercise.

Please complete this exercise before continuing to the next chapter.

Sit down in a comfortable position. Smile! Place a real, genuine smile of happiness on your face. Close your eyes. Relax your mind and body by taking long, slow, deep breaths. Relax. Breathe in, breathe out. Focus on your breathing. Feel the rise and fall of your chest and stomach. Continue this until the activity of your mind stops. No questions, no wondering, no worries, just breathing, relaxing, smiling, existing, aware.

Knowing Your Purpose

This is a state of essentially no mind; no thoughts or Self-talk. Continue to focus on your breathing, in and out, in and out. You should gradually slip into a peaceful, relaxed, calm state. Take as long as necessary for any thoughts or bodily sensations to slowly fade away into the background or cease completely if only for a few seconds. Just allow them to come and go and return the focus of your attention to your breathing. Breathe in, long and deep, breathe out. Breathe in, even longer and deeper, breathe out.

Once you are able to achieve a state of mind without any thoughts, without any sensory distractions or create a "gap" of awareness, you are there. This is your Self existing in its natural state. No thoughts, free of tension, fear, boredom, or any other negative state. Existing as if you were floating in space — being still. Can you feel it? Sense it? Just calm and steady; letting things be as they are, at peace, at rest. Some call this a meditative state.

Experience this state of being as long as you like then slowly start to come out of it. Open your eyes to the external world while continuing to breathe deeply and slowly.

If you find this difficult because you are unable to slow down or stop the mental activity in your mind, try this technique recommended by Eckhart Tolle. He says to ask your Self a question and wait for an answer. There will be a "gap" of awareness that allows stillness to come into your mind during the period of time you are waiting for an answer.

The question to ask your Self is: "I wonder what my next thought will be?" You will find that your mind will

The Evaluation of Self Test

become still and aware. It will wait for an answer. This is your Self that resides in the background of all the mental activity in your mind.

Take a five to ten minute break afterward to observe your Self and answer the following questions before continuing. Complete the exercise now. This is an important evaluation point.

Did this help you in any way? Were you able to experience your natural state? Has anything changed within you? Are you more relaxed and at ease with the world around you? How long did it take for your thinking mind to take over? Observe your thoughts. What kind of thoughts seem to have been dominant? How and/or why has your state of being changed since you opened your eyes? How does your interaction with the world around you affect your ability to remain in this state? How can you respond differently to the world around you to remain in this state most of the time?

Now that you have had a chance to experience the natural state of your Self, your natural state of being, let's examine it further. We will work from the inside out — from your internal state of being to the external situations you have created.

You Are a Creative Force

When I think about the purpose of my Self, I relate to it from a spiritual, universal perspective. In the beginning, there was a creative force. Most people refer to this creative force as God. This force created the infinite universe and all other living creations within it. We were

Knowing Your Purpose

created as singular, individual beings from this creative force.

Everything this force creates is an individualization of it Self; so everything it creates is creative. We as human beings are creative through our thoughts, emotions, voice, and body. The purpose of this creative force within us is to create while existing as physical beings until our physical life ends.

But our creativity can get out of control without a period of evaluation to determine what we are creating. This lack of control is common in a lot of people so it seems natural when our thoughts, feelings, words and physical actions create situations we don't like or want. But you can control, direct, and guide these elements of your Self when you have a purpose for your creative force; a purpose for your existence as a creative being.

So the question is: How will you exist as this creative force, this creative being that you are? The answer to this question is important to recognize so that you will know how to direct the creative force within you. Will you exist as a peaceful being that lives in harmony with the universe? Will you exist as a destructive force that wreaks havoc in the world around you? Will you exist as an emotionally sensitive being that is fearful and withdrawn? Will you exist as a being of love that cares for others?

Write an answer to these questions: How would you describe the way you are existing now? In what way are you using your creative force to your advantage and disadvantage? Write your answer out in as much detail as

The Evaluation of Self Test

necessary to evaluate your unique situation. This is an important evaluation point.

Your Natural State of Being

We all should be able to exist in our natural state of being at any time. But in order to do this, we must learn how to control our mind and stop thinking at any time we wish. We must also be able to remove the flow of undesirable, unproductive emotional energy from our state of being at any time, in any situation.

You will find that taking long, slow, deep breaths while smiling is a good method to use in calming and settling your Self and your body enough to achieve your natural state.

Remember: Existing in your natural state is where your creative force resides. And your natural state provides four significant benefits. They are:

1. The universal creative force, God, will speak to you from the stillness of your natural state. "Be still and know I am God."
2. Creativity resides in the stillness of your natural state – return here at any time in any situation especially negative, problematic ones.
3. Solutions often arise from your subconscious mind from the stillness of your natural state.
4. Negative emotions/states of being such as fear, anger, anxiety, doubt, depression, etc. cannot exist in your natural state. They dissolve and fade away.

Knowing Your Purpose

Remember, we are focused on being and existing, not on having. You can exist in your natural state regardless of what you have or don't have. But you may not be able to exist in this natural state if the opposite were true. You may be fortunate enough to have all the things of this world such as money, fame, fancy cars, a big home, a perfect job or relationships and so on. But you may still repeatedly exist in an unbalanced, discontented state of being as a result of negative thoughts and emotions related to the situations in your life.

Don't get me wrong though, nice things are nice to have. Just don't become overly attached to them. Because if you are more concerned about having, your happiness will come and go as people, places, and things come and go to and from your life. Existence and being are internal and eternal; having is only external.

So are you more concerned about being or having? This is an important evaluation point. Our reference point for a purpose is focused on being instead of having. Your state of being is more important than anything you may temporarily have. It's unfortunate but I would say most people don't realize this until hardship or tragedy hits them or some of the situations we pointed out earlier occur in their life.

This is because most of us project our Self into the things we have. We become attached to and sometimes obsessed with people, places, or things. This can lead to an attitude of "I have this, I have that." Or, "I need this and gotta have that to feel good about my Self or my life. Look at me and what I have. I'm better than you because I have this and that."

The Evaluation of Self Test

We go about our day to day lives working, getting paid and getting involved in various situations. We meet people, travel to places near and far, and we buy and do things we think will make us happy. We watch TV, eat, sleep and do it all over again the next day. And for some reason, we can find ourselves existing in an unhappy state more often than we want to.

Some of the Buddhists teachings describe this as "suffering". And we can suffer every day with these feelings, wondering, is this all there is to life? And if we are focused more on having instead of being, then yes, that is all there is.

But you can maintain a greater sense of Self when you focus on being rather than projecting your Self into the things of this world or basing your life on what you have. Now let's review some added benefits of existing and living with a purpose for your Self.

Benefits of Having a Purpose

One benefit of a purpose for your Self is that it shifts your attention. Your attention is shifted in the direction of achieving your purpose. Any aspect of your mental thought process, mindset or character that does not fall in line with your purpose must be changed.

A mental shift in your thought process occurs so that you resolve any issues that conflict with your purpose when they first arise. You will no longer allow a minor issue to become a major problem. This is because your desire is to focus your time and energy on what you want, not what you don't want.

Knowing Your Purpose

Another benefit of having a purpose is that it builds confidence in the actions you take. For example, have you ever done something that didn't turn out well? And when asked, "Why did you do that?" your first response was, "I didn't do it on purpose."

Your purpose gives you the confidence to state, "Yes, I did that on purpose." You don't make excuses when the outcomes of your actions don't turn out well. Mistakes will be made but you don't get defensive. Apologies, as well as forgiveness, are given freely. You are ready to deal with any situation, whether it becomes a source of conflict or not, in a confident Self-assured manner.

And a purpose provides focus. Rick Warren said that, "knowing your purpose focuses your life. It concentrates your effort and energy on what's important." I once read an article that described how critical your focus can be when you are driving. It stated that when you learn to drive a race car, one of the first things you're taught is to focus on the direction in which you want to go.

If your car gets a little out of control, the one thing you must avoid, at all cost, is to look at and focus on what you are afraid of. If you focus on the wall or another car, the likelihood of you crashing goes up by 1000 %. Almost without fail, you tend to steer in the direction of what you focus on, whether you want to or not. This same principle applies to what you focus on in your life.

When deciding what the primary focus of your attention will be, remember you are trying to:

1. F - Focus on
2. O - One purpose for your Self

The Evaluation of Self Test

3. C - to Concentrate on
4. U - while resisting the Urges and distractions that life presents you
5. S - as the Situations in your life align with your purpose

In addition to the benefits listed above, each letter of the word "Purpose" has meaning as it relates to the benefits that existing in your natural state can provide. Your purpose will refresh your Personality; it will take you to a new level of Understanding of the situations in your life and allow you to Renew your commitment and reengage your Self in the process of your personal development. It will help you to become Patient with your Self and others.

It will enable you to Observe your reactions so you can respond differently to the people and situations that draw you away from your purpose so you can immediately Seize control of any negative thoughts or emotions that may arise. This will allow you to remain an Enthusiastic and energetic creator of your own purposeful existence.

- **P**ersonality
- **U**nderstanding
- **R**enew / **R**eengage
- **P**atience
- **O**bservation
- **S**eize
- **E**nthusiasm

Knowing Your Purpose

Personality — Your Personality will be refreshed and renewed when it is a reflection of your purpose. It will change as a natural result of living in accordance with your purpose. This natural shift in character occurs as you approach the situations in your life with a new mindset.

This will require you to let go of some old thoughts and ideas you have become attached to or have conformed to. This is because they are a part of the repetitious choices and decisions that may have caused unwanted situations to evolve to their current status.

This shift in your personality should be obvious to anyone you consider a close friend or relative. If you or others do not notice a change in your personality you should wonder if anything has really changed. You might be fooling your Self into believing change has occurred when it really hasn't.

Understanding — Your purpose will take you to a new level of understanding of your Self and other people. Changing any aspect of your Self or your life is a difficult process that takes time. It can be a slow task that challenges and frustrates you. It is said that, "You can't change people, you can only change your Self." It should be said, "Until you can change your Self, don't expect other people to change." C. G. Jung said, "Everything that irritates us about others can lead us to an understanding of ourselves."

We often complain about other people's actions and behaviors and fail to realize we have our own share of faults that other people wish we would change. But we

The Evaluation of Self Test

don't. We can't see our own faults but we can easily point out the faults of others.

It isn't until you experience the process of change for your Self that you come to understand just how hard it really is. But once you do, you can sympathize with anyone who has ever tried to change and understand those that never make an attempt.

Your attention will become more focused on your own attempts to change and less on what others are not doing. And rather than being critical of others, you will understand why other people choose to remain in the comfort zone of conformity. Your own journey through the process of change will help open your mind to other styles of living and thinking. You will come to understand that just because you can't agree with another person on each other's lifestyle and thinking doesn't make either of you wrong, just different.

Renew / Reengage — Periodically, you will find it necessary to renew your commitment to living with the purpose you have chosen. In the beginning, it may be very difficult to remain engaged in the process 100% of the time. Situations may arise that demand your attention. These situations may distract you long enough for you to fall back into old patterns of thinking and behavior. It can be anything that temporarily shifts your attention and focus away from your purpose. These types of situations cannot be predicted or anticipated.

But no matter what the situation is, at some point, you will have an opportunity to renew your commitment to your purpose or continue to drift away from it. These will

Knowing Your Purpose

be important evaluation points in your life. These will be times for decisions to be made. It will be easy to continue to live in a situation that distracts you and move on to another. Your old thought patterns will resurface to convince you that your actions are justified. Excuse after excuse will arise in your mind.

This is the time to reengage. This is when you must remember your purpose and all of the long term benefits it will provide. It will be easy to begin again and renew your commitment to the process of change you are undergoing if the fulfillment of your purpose is important to you.

Patience — You will need to make numerous decisions in order to succeed in your attempt to change your life. One such decision will be to decide whether or not to demonstrate patience during the process of change. You will need to be patient with your Self and others as your lifestyle begins to shift into alignment with your purpose. There will be countless occasions when your patience will be tested and you must make a choice.

One of your biggest tests will be to simply be patient while you wait; wait on the pain to end, decisions to be made, the next day, your situation or Self to change. A few others will be to wait in line, in traffic, for food or service, people, and so on. But no matter what the situation is, you will be presented with two options:

Option one, you can choose to be patient.
Option two, you can choose to be impatient.

The Evaluation of Self Test

One option will allow you to move toward your purpose. The other will move you away from it. Let's face it — trying to live in your natural state or close to it will not be easy. It will be a challenge from the start. And if you continually allow your Self to become impatient, you will only add to any frustrations you may experience during the change process.

Every challenging situation or troublesome person that you encounter will be an opportunity to practice patience. I use the word "practice" because being patient will be a continuous learning experience that you may never fully master. Each encounter will affect you differently. It will involve different people, in different places, at different times that draw upon different emotions. So be mindful that you may respond differently each time.

But with each encounter, you will have an opportunity to practice patience. You will also receive the added benefit of building upon a foundation for Self-control and discipline. These qualities will serve you well if your old thought patterns begin to slip back into your mind.

These qualities will also help if you begin to doubt your ability to actually change your life by changing your Self. Your desire to change may be doomed to fail from the start if you cannot demonstrate the qualities of patience, Self-control, and discipline. Always keep in mind that living with a better state of being is possible if you can practice patience in all situations.

Knowing Your Purpose

Observation — Your power of observation will increase each day that you experience your purpose. The increase may be so gradual that it may go unnoticed for weeks. The slow and steady increase in your observational power will allow you to approach situations with a fresh point of view. You will see your surroundings from a new perspective that is based on your purpose.

Your surroundings and the people you frequently encounter will become a source for new ideas and experiences instead of a source of boredom or conformity. This is because your mind's eye will be focused on ways to bring your purpose into your experience in the present moment. You will be more observant of situations that are likely to move you toward or away from your natural state. This will enable you to experience the situation in a way that better suits your purposeful needs.

As your power of observation increases, you will become more observant of your own behavior and of the behavior of those around you. This will create an intuitive knowing of the right decisions and actions to take in all situations to bring order into your life. You will be able to "see" what is required to continue the process of change to improve your situation.

Everything will seem to have a freshness about it. This will be a sign that you are breaking free from your old Self and creating a new one. It may be uncomfortable at times and you will find your Self wondering what is going on. This is normal so don't be surprised. But with each new observation made, you will move toward your purposeful desires and achieve the goals you will select later on.

Seize Control — To live a life with purpose you must seize control of your thoughts and emotions on a continuous basis. Your thoughts are creative. Whatever you think about most (internally) is what you will ultimately create in your life (externally). You must take hold of the ideas that spring from your mind and use only those that will enable you to live with your purposeful intentions. Any thought that is in opposition to your purpose must be ignored and disregarded.

Thoughts are often repetitious in nature. Negative thoughts are like a repeated assault by an enemy. Each time they occur you must seize control of them. You must turn them away by choosing to think about what it is you want, not what you don't want. You could also spend time analyzing why the thought even occurred. This may help neutralize it. But your time and effort will be better spent if you focus on your purpose.

This same effort must also be applied to your emotions. Emotions are also creative. Just observe the chaos that is caused by a person that displays anger, resentment, depression, paranoia or any other negative emotion. You can clearly see the need to seize control of these emotions even when you feel they are justified. They will only serve to undermine your efforts to change.

You must continually stay alert to your mood as it changes throughout each day. One minor irritation can trigger any number of negative thoughts and emotions. It's not a matter of if you will have a negative thought or

Knowing Your Purpose

emotion, it's when and how many. Your job is to seize the moment and channel any negative energy experienced into something positive.

In most situations though, all it may take is some time to pass until your mood changes. Nobel Peace prize winner Thomas Mann said, "Time cools, time clarifies: no mood can be maintained quite unaltered through the course of hours." You will be able to reduce the effects of the negative thoughts and emotions you experience as your ability to seize control of them improves.

Remember: you must seize control of all of your thoughts and emotions until every aspect of your life is working toward the improvement of your life and the fulfillment of your purpose.

Enthusiasm — Your ability to maintain a high level of enthusiasm and energy, most of the time, will be a key factor during your purposeful journey. Most people cannot maintain a high level every day. This is natural and is to be expected.

When most people cannot maintain a high level naturally, they use substitutes for stimulation such as energy drinks and coffee or drugs and alcohol. Substitutes are helpful but it may be a sign that you need to relax and re-energize your mind and body by existing in your natural state.

You can clear the clouds of depression, sadness, hopelessness, or boredom that situations often bring when you exist in your natural state. Your enthusiasm and energy will last longer and longer and your low periods will become shorter and shorter with each day that you

The Evaluation of Self Test

do. You will find that all it takes is a little rest and relaxation to cure these short periods of low energy.

But through all of it, embrace the moment that is now. Staying in the moment, even as you read this, everything is as fresh and exciting as you make it. You must reduce the effects that external forces have on your level of enthusiasm and energy. Make each moment the best it can be.

Make this reading enjoyable and not a task. Enthusiasm breeds energy and excitement. Approach each situation with the attitude that each action you take, in each moment, you are actually experiencing your purpose.

You should be able to look back and say, "There were some good moments and some not so good moments but I enjoyed the excitement and challenges that each moment brought while I experienced my purpose."

How to Know You Are Living with Purpose

It's easy to say you are living with purpose. But the question is, how do you know when you are living with purpose? How would someone else visually recognize that you are living with purpose? First, when you start reaping some of the benefits we discussed earlier, even if it's only one, you will know the process of change has begun. Your internal state of being is undergoing a change. Second, these changes will slowly begin to manifest externally in your appearance and attitude in one or more of these areas as well as many others.

Knowing Your Purpose

Appearance

1. You may change your style of clothing
2. You may begin to smile more often to your Self or around others
3. You may change your hair, including your hairstyle, mustache, beard, eyebrows
4. You may change your makeup or stop wearing any at all
5. Your physique may change as a result of eating healthier and exercising
6. Your communication skills may change; talking less and listening more
7. Your gait / posture may change as you hold your head higher and walk with confidence

Attitude

1. You may become less concerned with what other people think or what you think they think
2. Negative emotions will have less of an effect on your state of being
3. You may become more approachable, responsive, open minded, and engaging
4. You may become more definite in your choices and decisions
5. You may look people in the eye more
6. You may become more knowledgeable professionally and in your personal situations
7. Your activity, productivity, and energy level may increase
8. You may become more affectionate in your personal relationships

The Evaluation of Self Test

You should reevaluate the actions you have taken toward living with a purpose if you or no one else has observed a change in any of these or other areas. And take immediate action to change at least one aspect of your appearance or attitude. Something has to change in order for change to begin. And you will really believe change is occurring when you can see the change in your Self.

Personal Example

Something that I have observed with quite a few people is that they don't know what they want so they live their lives randomly, without purpose. They live day to day with whatever comes their way. I know this because I was one of those people. From as early as the day I graduated from high school to the day I made the decision to leave the workforce, I never really knew I needed a purpose, let alone a philosophy. Life seemed just fine without either.

And after working for over thirty-one years to help my employers achieve their purpose and goals, I still didn't know I needed my own once I retired.

When I first retired it was pretty easy to stay busy. I went to the movies, traveled, played golf, spent time with family and friends, and helped the "working people" out when I could. This satisfied my wants and needs for a while but after a few months, the old feelings of discontent soon returned.

They were similar to the ones I felt when I decided it was time to retire. I then began to question the decision I made to retire because I felt the same level of discontent as when I was working. I began to think, "I could have kept working. Maybe I made a mistake."

I then felt like I needed something to work on to fill my time just like when I was working. So I began to write. And after writing for a few months off and on, writing became my therapy. It gave me a way to express my creative Self in a similar manner as when I worked.

It also provided me with a way to explore my Self internally — my thoughts, emotions, feelings, beliefs, and ideas. I also began to listen to some audio programs I had accumulated. Some of my favorites are Eckhart Tolle, Brian Tracy, Jim Rohn, Zig Ziglar, and Abraham Hicks to name a few. It was from Eckhart Tolle that I became more and more interested in living in the moment and understanding more about my Self.

Over time, I read about and began practicing some meditative techniques to explore this subject more. It was during a meditative session that I felt the most happiness and peace within my Self. It was during a meditative state that I experienced what I now recognize as my natural state of being. It was during a meditative session that I discovered what I eventually chose as the purpose for my Self.

At no time did I experience any negative emotions; no fear, guilt, doubt, worry or discontent during this meditative session. I decided I wanted to experience this state of being every day. And that is how I chose my purpose statement. I decided my purpose would be:

"To Exist as a Being of Happiness and Peace."

The Evaluation of Self Test

It's that simple. I can experience my purpose every day, in any activity I participate in. And I can do it without having to sit and focus intently to achieve my natural state. This is because I chose a state of mind as my purpose. That state of mind is "to exist as a being of happiness and peace." This is how I feel when I am in my natural state — what I experience and what I want to project into the world around me.

There is nothing in me that can prevent me from existing in this state whenever I want. It is for my own good so I don't allow my thoughts or emotions to block this state of mind from my experience. And yes there are always a few challenging days, situations, and experiences that can cause my state to change for short periods of time. But as Brian Tracy likes to emphasize, I exist in and experience my purpose "most of the time." And over time, so can you.

Create Your Purpose Statement

This Personal Development Solution asks the question: What purpose have you established for your Self? Your state of being? What answer did you write down earlier, if any? Here is my answer:

To exist in my natural state of being on a daily basis.

This natural state is different for everyone but will be similar at its core. So I want you to create and personalize your purpose statement now. Describe your natural state.

What did you experience or feel during the exercise you completed earlier? Describe your Self when you

Knowing Your Purpose

existed in your natural state. Describe how you want to exist. As a being that does what? As a being of what? That feels what? Experiences what?

Describe the state you would like to return to during the worst of times; when you are experiencing your most emotionally negative states of being. When boredom sets in. Describe the natural state of existence that will bring you out of the deepest states of depression.

Think this over for a while until a purpose statement comes to you. Go to your natural state and see if the answer comes to you. Your purpose statement for your Self will be complete once you can clearly describe how you feel and/or what you experience in your natural state of existence.

It should be related to a state of mind, a frame of mind, a system of thought that describes what you experience in your natural state of being. Create a statement that will provide direction to your creative thoughts, feelings, words, and physical actions when you go about your day to day activities.

Take your time when deciding and be patient with your Self. The decision should flow from within you naturally and with ease. Once you have written your purpose, you should be able to experience it immediately.

Your only challenge to experiencing your purpose as soon as you decide will be how well you are able to direct and control the creative force that resides within you; how well you can direct your thoughts, control your emotions, and manage your sensory perceptions.

Once you have made a choice and final decision on your purpose, type it up and keep it in a location where

The Evaluation of Self Test

you can see it regularly. You can also add it to your phone/tablet via one of the many apps that are available for a daily source of inspiration. Your purpose should be read or stated by the voice in your head on a daily basis until it is ingrained in your state of mind so it can be continually brought into your experience.

Summary

"Knowing your purpose gives meaning to your life, simplifies your life, motivates your life and prepares you for eternity." Rick Warren, *A Purpose Driven Life*.

Your purpose is about your ability to exist in your natural state at any time, in any place, in any situation. It is about existing as a creative being for as long as your physical life lasts. And it is about providing direction to the creative force within you to create situations that are in alignment with your purpose.

Your purpose statement should describe what you experience or feel when you are in your natural state. Your purpose will be easier to experience when your thoughts are focused on what you want, not what you don't want. This will create a state of mind that is attentive, confident, and focused.

Your purpose will allow for the creation of new thoughts and ideas that will refresh your Personality, increase your Understanding of the situations you create, and Renew your commitment to your personal development.

Knowing Your Purpose

Your purpose will also provide you with the Patience you need to slow down and Observe new ways to respond so you can Seize control of any situation that may arise in a purposeful and Enthusiastic manner.

Exercise

For now, let us reinforce your ability to experience your natural state of existence as a creative being. Read over the directions first and perform this exercise again.

Close your eyes. Sit down in a comfortable position. Smile. Relax your mind and body by taking long, slow deep breaths. Relax. Breathe in, breathe out. Focus on the breaths. Feel the rise and fall of your chest and stomach. Continue this until the activity of your mind stops. No questions, no wondering, just breathing, relaxing, smiling, existing, aware.

This is a state of essentially no mind; no thoughts or Self-talk. Focus on your breathing, in and out, in and out. You should gradually slip into a peaceful, relaxed, calm state. Take as long as necessary for any thoughts or bodily sensations to slowly fade away into the background or cease completely if only for a few seconds. Use the techniques of asking your Self "the question" I recommended earlier if necessary.

At the point the activity of your mind stops, no matter how short the period or "gap" is, you are existing in your natural state of being. Once you reach your natural state of being, of no mind, no thought, in a totally relaxed state, remain in this state for as long as you like. Once you are ready, open your eyes and try to remain in this

The Evaluation of Self Test

state. Your face should have a look and underlying feeling of happiness, Self-assurance, and Self-confidence. Physically calm, yet ready to act while existing in the "gap".

From this central point of reference is where you want your response to the world around you to emanate from. This allows you to operate in harmony with the creative force within you. To operate and cooperate with God.

Complete the exercise now.

Knowing Your Purpose

Quiz One

Answer all of the questions on a sheet of paper or in your journal. Answer them to the best of your ability. And remember there are no wrong answers. What you write is for your benefit.

1. My purpose statement is _____.
2. Why did you choose this purpose?
3. If you already had a purpose, did you change it and why? Why not?
4. How will this purpose affect your life?
5. What is the first purposeful action you will take to begin the change process?
6. Who will be the primary person to support you during this process?
7. What have you learned about your Self by choosing this purpose?
8. What benefits of having a purpose will have the greatest impact on your Self?
9. What must you start and stop doing in order to live a life with purpose?
10. What have you learned about your Self that you didn't know prior to reading this chapter?
11. Do you think having is more important than your state of being? Why?

The Evaluation of Self Test

Relax.

Smile.

Complete the prerequisite before continuing to the next chapter.

Chapter Three

Understanding Your Life Situations Part One

Aligning Your Life Situations With Your Purpose

You are now ready to evaluate whether or not your current situations are in alignment with your purpose. You now have to evaluate if the situations you have created are a true reflection of how you want to live while you exist with your decided purpose. You must now evaluate each situation in your life to identify where change is or is not needed and determine what needs to change within your Self in order to transform them.

In this chapter, we will define and discuss life situations and provide a method for you to evaluate and manage them more effectively. You will then create your philosophy. Your philosophy will be your plan of action for living a purposeful life. The principles contained within your philosophy will help solidify the change that is needed within your Self to align your existing and future situations with your purpose.

But before we begin, let me forewarn you now: this will be the most challenging part of your evaluation. This is where the hard work starts. This is where your test really begins. The situations you currently find your Self existing in will present the second hardest obstacle to overcome in order for you to experience your purpose at any time. The first, of course, will be your Self.

The Evaluation of Self Test

Situations will often push and pull at every corner of your being. They can cause a roller coaster of mental activity, cause you to be emotionally unpredictable, cause physical stress and cause you to question your faith.

Now that you have been forewarned, don't let this knowledge prevent you from completing your evaluation and passing the test. Let it motivate you even more to overcome it. So are you ready? Great! Let's begin your second Personal Development Solution, Understanding your Life Situations.

Categories of Life Situations

By now, you might be wondering what exactly your life situation is. What answer did you come up with? Write down what you think your life situation is in as much detail as you can. Take as long as you need to write this out. It doesn't have to be written perfectly, just get the information down on paper. We will compare what you have written to my definition in a moment. This is an important evaluation point. Do this now.

All done? Remember, no cheating on the test. Okay, here is my definition: It is the current state of every situation you feel is important in your life and your attitude towards it. Specifically, it is what you think and how you feel about these situations at this moment in time. Your life situation is all of the situations you find your Self in today, in every area of your life.

As an example, your overall life situation could be broken down into sections or categories similar to the way

Understanding Your Life Situations Part One

information is entered for a profile on any website or the information you would enter on an application. Such as:

a. Health: 32 years old, six feet in height, weight is one hundred ninety pounds, exercise 2-3 times a week, plays soccer and tennis, chronic back pain
b. Marital: married, seven years, two children, completed three sessions of marriage counseling
c. Employment: employed, same company for 10 years, good benefits, two performance/attendance warnings
d. Financial: earning $50,000 a year, mortgaging a single family home, $25,000 in credit card debt, behind in payments on one credit card and one loan
e. Education: Enrolled in college, taking two courses at night, $20,000 in student loan debt
f. Religious: a member of a Baptist church, attends occasionally, spouse attends another church

This would give the average person a general idea of what your overall life situation is at the moment. You can get even more detailed but this should give you a general idea of how to determine what your individual life situations are, that, together, form your life situation. How does your answer compare to this?

To help you develop a better understanding of your life situation, take a few minutes now and write out the various situations you are involved in at this moment in time. Use categories to separate them. Try to stay away from the story of how each situation developed for now. Just focus on the situation as it stands at this moment. Later on, you will use

The Evaluation of Self Test

this information to evaluate the details of each situation and your attitude toward it to deepen your understanding of the people, places, and things that are involved.

To help get you started with this exercise, use the following Categories of Life Situations. Feel free to add more as necessary.

1. Relationships (family, marital, business, friends, etc.)
2. Financial
3. Health
4. Employment / Career
5. Environment (Work, Home, etc.)
6. Spiritual / Religion
7. Education / Personal Development
8. Recreation or Leisure

Problematic Life Situations

You should now have a great idea of the status of your various life situations. So, how do you feel about your life situation as a whole? Good, bad, happy, or sad? What kind of emotions does thinking about individual situations produce? Positive or negative? What are the situations you like and don't like? What situations are in alignment with your purpose and which ones are not?

During this exercise, you may have realized there are some situations that require more of your time and attention than you have been giving them. They may have even caused anger or tension within you by just writing them down. These are the types of situations that produce

Understanding Your Life Situations Part One

negative emotions whenever you think about them. They also move the focus of your attention away from your purpose. These are the situations that must be brought into alignment with your purpose. These are the situations that may need a principle added to your philosophy to help resolve them. These are problematic life situations.

In his book, *Journey into Your Self*, Eckhart Tolle states that for the most part, life situations are "problematic" and if they are not now, "give it a little time." You will find that the life situations that frequently preoccupy your thoughts and cause the most negative emotions to surface within you are the most problematic.

Having at least one problematic life situation is typical for most people. How many do you have? The difference between the person that can experience their purpose most of the time and the person that cannot is how they handle these situations as they arise. This is the key.

The person that exists within their purpose has learned how to manage the various situations in their life better; with less stress, anger, fear, or worry. They manage problematic situations with a level of understanding that produces solutions to resolve issues or conflicts rather than feed into the negative energy the situation may produce.

You must be continually mindful of problematic life situations as they arise. This is when you must bring some of the benefits of living with purpose into whatever you are experiencing. Immediate action must be taken to resolve whatever created the situation. Focus on the root cause of the problematic situation instead of the effects. This will prevent it from becoming more problematic than it should be or could become.

The Evaluation of Self Test

And of course, there will be some problematic life situations that you just can't muster up the courage to address. Let's face it, some situations will be emotionally difficult to confront. Do you have any? What are they? Some people are difficult to approach, some places and things are hard to let go of. It is then that you must have the courage to face your fears.

You must determine what is preventing you from addressing the issue. Is it fear, worry, doubt, or a limiting belief? Is it love? Or is it that you don't want to hurt someone's feelings even though you are sacrificing your own?

You must prepare your Self to deal with the consequences of any decision you make. Resolving the issue could mean the end of your marriage, the loss of your job, your home, bankruptcy, or even serving a sentence of jail time. You must figure out what you must do, can do, and you are willing to do.

You have to keep chipping away at the issues involved in the situation until it is resolved. No matter what it is though, you must overcome it. You must take action to resolve it or it will be a continuous source of discontent that produces negative emotions and continuous thoughts that distracts you from your purpose.

Problematic life situations have certain characteristics in common that you should be mindful of. They are:

1. They move the focus of your attention and your emotional state away from your purpose.
2. They conflict with one or more of the principles listed in your philosophy.

3. They are or can become an obstacle to achieving your goals.
4. They are void of love; they are heavy laden with negative emotions.
5. They generate a continuous stream of repetitive, unwanted, mostly negative thoughts.

Cross Connected Categories of Life Situations

Every category of your life situation is connected. Your financial category is connected to your relationship category which is connected to your employment category which is cross connected back to your financial category and so on.

A good cross connected example would be, your employment fuels your finances, which helps you support your family which allows you to take a vacation and tithe at church. Most people can easily exist within their purpose in this simple example.

However, bills can accumulate, vacation plans may have to be canceled, your spouse may have to stop working to care for you, and your kids may have to drop out of college if you cannot go to work because of a long term disability. It will naturally be harder to experience your purpose in this example. This is how problematic cross connected categories can have a negative impact on your life.

The more cross connections there are in your life that are not problematic, the better your overall life situation will be and the easier it will be for you to experience your purpose. The opposite is also true. The more problematic

The Evaluation of Self Test

cross connected categories you have, the more problematic your overall life situation will be and it will be harder to experience your purpose.

I'm not saying that you can't exist in your natural state, only that it may become harder to do so because of the number of cross connected, problematic life situations you are experiencing at one time.

You must continually maintain awareness of how all of your Categories of Life Situations impact one another. Without awareness, you could make a decision regarding a situation in one category that leads to the creation of a problematic situation in another.

In situations where you have several problematic cross connected categories of life situations, prioritize each situation by category first. Then resolve the situation that will have the biggest positive impact on all categories. You can then work your way down your prioritized list on the others.

Sometimes all it will take is for you to resolve your top two or three problematic situations and everything else will resolve itself. Just remember to stay mindful of how a change in one category can or will impact another at some point in time.

Situation Management

Situation management is the process of managing each of your life situations with the time and attention that is necessary to align them with your purpose. The most effective way to do this is to simply bring the mindset of your purpose into each situation. In addition, the benefits of

Understanding Your Life Situations Part One

having a purpose such as, confidence, focus, patience, understanding, enthusiasm, etc. are the tools that will help you align your most problematic situations with your purpose.

It starts with situational awareness. You can manage your situations more effectively when you are aware of how your daily experiences conflict with the mindset of your purpose. In most situations, you will "feel" the impact before you "know" the impact. It's about sensing, feeling, experiencing the situation as if it is a part of you. Because it really is. Anything you experience from your mind, body, emotions, and spirit is a part of you.

For example, if we use the purpose statement of, "existing as a being of happiness and peace," when a situation produces a negative emotion (anger, fear, jealousy, worry, hatred, etc.) you will know almost immediately that the situation is moving you away from your purpose — away from your mindset of existing with happiness and peace.

It is at that moment that you must bring the mindset of your purpose into the situation and let all of its benefits guide you. Awareness produces patience which will give you time to pause before you react to what you are experiencing. This creates an opportunity to change how you would normally respond, especially when this response would not be in alignment with your purpose.

Your feelings aren't perfect so this may not be true in all situations. Let your intuition be your guide. But in most situations, how you feel about what you are experiencing is a signal for you to pay attention, to be mindful of what is going on. Have your feelings or intuition ever signaled you

The Evaluation of Self Test

and you ignored it and, as a result, a problematic situation occurred?

You must also be aware of your situational expectations. We give little thought to our expectations prior to a planned event or situation most of the time. We normally expect everything to go well. But when things do not turn out how we would like, it can lead to anger, confusion, disappointment, frustration, and problematic situations. Has this ever happened to you?

With this in mind, it is a good idea to write down what your expectations are. This is not necessary all the time. But in those cases where you feel a situation will conflict with your purpose, produce lasting negative emotions or create repetitive negative thoughts, write down your expectations prior to the situation occurring.

Once the situation is over, review your list to see what actually happened. Determine if your worst fears came true or if the situation turned out better than you expected. The purpose here is to become aware of the situations that trigger positive or negative thoughts or emotions.

This serves to help you understand more about your Self. To help you understand how you mentally, physically or emotionally react and verbally respond in certain situations with certain people in certain places doing certain things. You can then manage these situations with more awareness and more realistic expectations in the future.

Understanding Your Life Situations Part One

Four Phases of Situation Management

Situation Management is also a decision-making process. It is a four phase process that you may already be using but not consciously aware of. The four phases are:

1. Opportunities for Change
2. Making Conscious Choices
3. Making the Final Decision
4. Monitoring and Evaluating the New Situation

You must learn how to take advantage of the opportunities available to you in order to manage your life situations more effectively. As opportunities arise, you can weigh your options and make a conscious choice as it relates to the situation. Once you have made your choice, you can resolve in your mind that you have made your final decision, without regrets.

This will implant your decision into your subconscious mind as what you want, what you desire. Your subconscious, which is the stillness that resides within your Self, will then provide your conscious mind with ideas to help you manage the situation as it evolves.

But to make this happen, you must make a final decision. It is then that you can begin to take the actions necessary to align your life situations with your purpose. You will then need to simply monitor the situation and evaluate it as it evolves, as it changes, to make sure it meets your expectations. If not, repeat the four phases until the situation changes to your satisfaction.

The Evaluation of Self Test

When you initially start using the four phases of situation management, it may be necessary for you to follow them in a step by step, regimented manner. This will only be required until you have committed the phases to memory and have become proficient in each phase.

Opportunities for Change

The first phase of improving your situation management skills is recognizing opportunities as they present themselves and their related options. As I stated earlier, you must be aware of each situation in your life as new ones arise and existing ones change. This is where opportunities for positive change are often overlooked.

This is where action must be taken to control or adjust to the situation. You cannot hesitate, become passive, or procrastinate at the moment you become aware that a situation is changing especially if it is not in alignment with your purpose. Delay might allow great opportunities to pass that may not become available again. So you must take immediate, decisive action to double or even triple the number of options available to you.

For example, you have been working toward the completion of your college degree for the past three years by completing classes at night. You have one more class to finish and then you will be graduating. Your life situation is about to change.

More specifically, you could say your education situation is about to change. You can take control of this changing situation, this opportunity, by doing one of several things: updating your resume, applying for jobs

Understanding Your Life Situations Part One

inside your current company or others, changing your letterhead or electronic signature to reflect the new degree, requesting a raise in salary, or you may want to begin researching a more advanced degree.

These are some of the options you now have as a result of getting your degree. Getting your degree will change your education situation and provide you with an opportunity to change your overall life situation. This opportunity will provide you with numerous options. All you have to do is act. Take action by making clear and conscious choices for positive changes to occur in your life.

Or, you could do nothing. By doing nothing you will celebrate the achievement at the graduation, have a party afterward with friends and family and then, hang the diploma on the wall. After that its business as usual; you fall right back into your regular routine of living.

But what has been the impact on your life situation? How has this change in your education changed some aspect of your life? When you examine it you will find that nothing has really changed. It didn't change because you didn't take advantage of the opportunity that getting your degree or rather changing your education situation provided you.

5W1H Method of Brainstorming

Sometimes additional options may not be readily known by you or anyone else. This is a good time to brainstorm. Brainstorming is the perfect way to find new opportunities and explore new options. By using what I refer to as the 5W1H Method of Brainstorming, you can

The Evaluation of Self Test

solve almost any problem in your life. This method isn't new. It has also been called the "Kipling Method" based on Rudyard Kipling's poem, "Six Honest Serving Men."

I have named it 5W1H to make it easier for me to remember when I need to recall it. Whenever I am faced with a situation or problem to resolve, my mind automatically recalls the 5W1H questions and I start the process of brainstorming. Hopefully, with use over time, it will work the same for you.

The method is simple. The easiest way to start is to ask your Self: Who, What, Where, When, Why and How as it relates to the situation or problem at hand. Some examples are provided below. You should, of course, create your own variation of the 5W1H questions as they relate to your unique situation.

1. Who – This includes the people involved: Who is responsible for this? Who can I talk to about it? Who can help me?
2. What – This is the action that is occurring or needs to occur: What is happening? What caused the situation? What else can I do? What action can I take to resolve this?
3. Where – This is the location the situation occurred or the place where the situation can be resolved: Where did this happen? Where can I get this resolved?
4. When – This is the time period the situation occurred or timeframe for some type of action: When did this situation start or end? When can I change the situation?

Understanding Your Life Situations Part One

5. Why – The reason the situation occurred or the purpose of some action taken: Why did this situation occur? Why didn't I take action to take advantage of this situation or prevent this situation from occurring? Why didn't I respond to the situation in a different manner?
6. How – This is the method used to improve, change or understand the situation: How did this happen? How can we change this situation? How can I respond differently to this type of situation? How is it impacting my life situation? How can it be resolved? How do I feel about it?

This method works twice as good if you have someone to help. Ask your spouse, a family member, a close friend or a coworker for their opinion. As they say "two heads are often better than one". Each person's point of view can be and often is different from our own. All of our life journeys and conditionings are unique.

We can all travel down the same road but see things completely different. I might be looking left when another person is looking right, up, down or maybe even have their eyes closed. Or our minds could be wandering into the past or future making everything at the moment a blur. This will make the other person's opinion and perception of the situation different. This "difference" can provide you with a set of options you may not have even considered.

Asking for help is always an option especially if you have special people in your life that will be honest with you - the kind of people that will tell you the truth and not just tell you what they think you want to hear. I prefer to have

The Evaluation of Self Test

people around me that will tell me the truth whether I like it or not. I believe we can always "agree to disagree".

I try to remember that while it may not be true for me, it may be true for them. Then I can try to apply their opinion to my situation to find new opportunities and options. Even strangers can be helpful especially if they have experience with the type of situation you find your Self in. Or you can simply have another person ask you the 5W1H questions to help you explore the situation as deeply and as thoroughly as possible.

So, by identifying a situation in its earliest stage of change, you can identify more opportunities to improve it. Use the 5W1H questions to find more opportunities and options when they seem limited. By doing this, you will have more choices available to improve your overall life situation. This will ultimately help you make better choices, more conscious choices.

Reflect on these questions for a few minutes: How many opportunities have you allowed to pass you by that could have changed a life situation for you? When did this happen? Where were you when it happened? Why didn't you act? Who could have helped you? What else could you have done to take advantage of the opportunity?

Making Conscious Choices

The second phase of Situation Management is making conscious choices based on the opportunities and options available to you. The choices you make in life are one of the single most important factors that determine the state of your life situations. If your life situations are not what or

Understanding Your Life Situations Part One

where you want them to be, a great place to start the process of change is in the choices you have been making.

Most people do not give any serious, conscious thought to the choices they make, especially to choices related to "matters of major importance". Choices related to matters of major importance are those that have a major impact on any category of your life situations such as your marriage, your job, your finances, health, etc.

"Matters of minor importance" are choices that the average person can easily make and change at any time and has little to no consequences as a result of the change such as what or where to eat.

Some people use their instinct when making choices. As Malcolm Gladwell says in his book, *Blink*, they make their choices in the "blink" of an eye. They sense the answer. Or you can say it comes from their conditioning. They have conditioned their Self to respond the same way, every day, in every type of situation. This can and does work most of the time for most people.

But when these conditioned choices continually create problematic situations or situations that are not in alignment with your purpose, a change has to be made.

Just about every book, movie or program on television uses the theme of choice. A choice has to be made over right or wrong or taking this or that direction in life. And we are shown what can happen with each choice that is made with good endings and not so good endings. Some choices even end in death.

One of the greatest books ever written that displays the impact choices can have in your life is the Bible. It is filled with good and bad in all types of situations. But having

The Evaluation of Self Test

read the sometimes tragic ending that can occur from the choices made by people in the Bible, people still make similar choices thinking, "That will never happen to me. That person didn't know what they were doing or how to do it the right way. I'm smarter." Some succeed, but quite a few find themselves in the same situation as the people they read about.

One of my favorite movies is *The Matrix*. In this film, people are connected to a software program, a virtual world. Everything works correctly 99.99999 percent of the time. There is only one problem: the programmer cannot figure out "human choice". Every so often the system crashes, killing almost everyone connected because someone makes a choice that could not be anticipated in the programming. The hero of the movie, Neo, is the only one other than the programmer to discover the problem. He clearly states, "The problem is choice."

Neo discovered that it is the unpredictable nature of what humans choose that is causing the situation that he finds himself in. And to complicate things even more for the programmer, Neo makes a choice that no one before him has ever made. To Neo's credit though, his choice solved the problem, or so we are left to believe.

The programmer can figure everything out except for what a person may choose in the numerous situations that life presents. What may be a perfect choice, the only choice for one person, may be the worst choice for another. This is played out in our lives every day.

Understanding Your Life Situations Part One

Your BEACH

Our goal here is not to solve the unpredictability of choice like in *The Matrix* (that may never be solved) but to assist you in making better choices, better choices related to the opportunities and options available to you.

By making better choices, you improve your Self and your life, reduce or eliminate problematic situations, and align all of your life situations with your purpose. And just as important, you'll make better, more conscious choices that lead to the improvement of your situation management skills.

We will accomplish our goal by focusing on the conditioning of your Self. This is where you will evaluate the details of each of your life situations and your attitude toward them. This will serve to help deepen your understanding of your Self, your life situations and of the people, places and things that are involved.

There are five areas of conditioning that we will focus on. They are:

1. Your **B**eliefs
2. Your **E**nvironment
3. Your **A**ctions
4. Your **C**onditioned Responses
5. Your **H**abits

We will call these areas your BEACH. You can change the conditioning of your Self if you change any area of your BEACH. You must recondition your Self — recondition your way of thinking, feeling, talking and acting. By doing this, you can break the cycle of your

The Evaluation of Self Test

repetitive choices to change the way you manage the situations in your life. You will have to look within your Self to determine the causes of your repetitive choices. You must take a long look in the mirror and gaze into your past behavior. This is the time to review your life story for clues. Find any and every thing that has led you to your current state of being and your current life situation.

This isn't something that you'll be able to do in a few minutes or even a day. It may take several days of honest Self-evaluation to determine what has been influencing the choices you have made in the past. But I recommend you limit the analysis to about three days.

This in-depth evaluation is only required once in order to establish a reference point for you to move forward from. With this knowledge in hand, you can dramatically change your future choices and your overall life situation.

So let's start there, at the BEACH. To change your BEACH, your conditioning, you must evaluate your beliefs and the environment in which those beliefs were formed as well as the places/locations you now frequent the most. In addition, you must evaluate your actions. Your actions demonstrate the choices you are making based on your beliefs and environment.

Next are your conditioned responses. You must evaluate how you have conditioned your Self to respond in basically the same way each time a particular type of situation arises. And finally, you must evaluate what has become habitual in your behavior that is good and not so good for you.

Before we begin, answer this question: Can you look in the mirror and take an honest look at how you have been

Understanding Your Life Situations Part One

behaving and make a choice to change wherever it is needed? If the answer is anything but yes, you should stop now. You will not be able to pass the test. Yes or no? Maybe is not an answer. When you are able to answer this question with a definitive YES, you can proceed. What is your answer? _____

You have now made your first conscious choice.

We will begin the evaluation of your BEACH with these directions in mind: First, choose a specific timeframe of your life to review. A timeframe from three months to three years is sufficient. You can go as far back as you feel is needed so that you can understand the motivation behind your past choices and what you were trying to achieve, if anything.

You may even choose to go back to your childhood. However, you may want to consider professional counseling if your conditioning is overly problematic and/or too deeply rooted.

Second, immediately change or eliminate any belief, environment, action, conditioned response, or habit that is in conflict with your purpose, continually contributes to the creation of problematic situations, or impedes your ability to improve a situation in your life or characteristic within your Self.

And third, use the 5W1H questions; who, what, where, when, why, and how, to question your Self about each area of your BEACH.

The Evaluation of Self Test

Beliefs

The first area of your BEACH is your beliefs. Your beliefs are the repetitious thoughts you have played so often that they have become the truth for you. It doesn't matter if these beliefs are based on facts, assumptions, or a feeling. These beliefs are true for you as they apply to the situations in your life.

Abraham Hicks, author of *Law of Attraction* said, "a belief is a thought you keep thinking," over and over again. Your beliefs are like a song that continually plays in the background of your mind at a low level. The question is, how did this song, these beliefs get implanted into your mind?

Some were formed from our teachers during the early years of our education while others were formed from our family, friends and other authority figures we encountered. Additionally, television, radio, movies, social media, and many other things have a tremendous amount of influence on what we believe now more than ever. And we are easily persuaded to believe this information without verifying its validity for ourselves.

But just because we believe certain things doesn't make them true. Your beliefs may be true for you but not someone else. Moreover, while some information may be true today, it may no longer be true at some point in the future. So why do we choose to continue believing certain things?

One answer is it's easy to just keep on believing in something because that's what you have always believed and everyone else you know believes it. It's your

Understanding Your Life Situations Part One

conditioning. Another is that once our beliefs are in place, they are difficult to change. Unfortunately, these are some of the reasons why we continue to make the same choices in the same situations.

We will begin by exploring all of your beliefs related to your matters of major importance in each of the situation categories, especially those that are problematic or are not in alignment with your purpose. For example, "What belief about my coworker is causing a problem at work? How can I change it? Who can help me? What do I believe about my financial situation prevents me from saving money? How can I change the situation? Where can I find employment to increase my earnings? How do I apply?"

In addition, ask your Self challenging questions such as, "Do I really believe I can change the problematic situations in my life? Do I believe I can respond differently to the opportunities I am given by making better choices? Do I really believe I can lose weight or do I believe I am destined to be overweight my entire life? Do I really believe I can quit smoking or do I believe it's too hard? Do I really believe I don't earn enough money to save? Do I believe I can discipline my Self and save ten percent of my earnings monthly?"

Make a list of at least ten beliefs from various categories of your life situations and challenge them. Question them until you can make a firm decision that they are true. If you cannot justify the belief, change it immediately to something that will help improve the choices you have been making in regards to it. Make a conscious choice to change the belief.

The Evaluation of Self Test

Humble your Self and admit you were wrong if necessary. Look for opportunities that a new belief will bring and start exploring the options that will be available to you. By changing just one belief, you can begin the process of changing your Self, making better choices and managing the situations in your life in a more efficient way.

Ask your Self, "What beliefs conflict with my purpose? What beliefs continually contribute to the creation or continuance of problematic situations? What beliefs impede my ability to improve/change a situation in my life or characteristic within my Self? Who can help me? When did these beliefs start? Why do I continue to believe them? How can I change these beliefs? What belief, if I change it today, will have the greatest impact on my Self and life immediately?"

Environment

The next area of your BEACH is your environment. Your environment is the location where you made your choices. And for this exercise, we are focusing mainly on the environments where problematic life situations were created. You must determine why these locations had a negative impact on your choices and life situation.

These locations might seem innocent at first glance but under closer scrutiny, you might find that your behavior in these environments creates problems you hadn't thought about before.

For example, going out on the town to socialize with friends is a nice, relaxing, and fun-filled activity. But you must evaluate if you are making bad choices when you go

Understanding Your Life Situations Part One

out by getting involved in bad relationships or drinking and driving? Are you making bad spending choices by going to the mall to "just look around" and then find your Self drowning in debt as a result of using credit cards? Do you always get angry in traffic and unknowingly get into arguments at work?

Where do you spend most of your time? What environment is taking away from the time you have available for matters of major importance or certain people in your life? What adjustments can be made? Can the time you spend there be reduced? An obvious place to start is at your place of employment. Another could be a room in your own home. Are you choosing to isolate your Self from others in this place of comfort?

Are you spending so much time isolated in your "place of comfort" surfing the internet, browsing social media, visiting chat rooms, or getting involved in online situations, that it is having a negative impact on your marriage, relationship with your children, or other aspects of your life situation?

In addition, how do your primary environments (home, work, etc.) look? What condition are they in? Are they clean, orderly, and free of clutter? If not, clean these areas immediately. Instill order in any environment you spend time where it does not already exist. Encourage others to do so if you are not able to. It's not about seeking perfection, just order.

Environments that are clean, orderly, and free of clutter promote good health, increase productivity, create space, reduces stress, and are more visually appealing and inspiring to spend time in.

The Evaluation of Self Test

Write down at least ten places that you spend the majority of your time and what you do there. Examine how these environments, the places you frequent the most, have impacted your choices. Make a conscious choice to change any environment that continually causes problems in your life today.

Even if it's simply moving your activities to another room in your home, this will move you out of your comfort zone and may help to improve a problematic situation. If you can't change a problematic environment immediately, make a plan and take decisive action to change it in the future.

Ask your Self, "What environments conflict with my purpose, continually contributes to the creation of problematic situations or impedes my ability to improve a situation in my life or characteristic within my Self? Who or what is at these locations that draw me to them? When did I start going to these locations? Why do I continue to go to these locations? Where else can I go? How can I stop going to these locations? What makes these locations so special and hard to stop frequenting? What environment, if I stop going there today, will have the greatest impact on my Self and life immediately?"

Actions

The next area of the BEACH for you to evaluate is your actions. Your actions may be the most important aspect of your BEACH. It is said by many that "your actions speak louder than your words" because your actions reflect the

Understanding Your Life Situations Part One

choices you have made. What do your actions say about your choices?

Think over some of the actions you took related to the matters of major of importance in each category of your life situations. Search those actions to discover any patterns of behavior, action by action. Do you take action without regard to consequences or to who else they may affect? Did you take action immediately when it was needed? Have you been doing what you said you would do? Are you a person of your word? Are you reliable, dependable?

Or did you make a choice and then delay or postpone your actions? Did you create excuses to delay actions or procrastinate for so long that your actions were not as effective as they could have been if taken earlier? Do you take time to consider your options and the pros and cons of each one before you act?

This does not have to take a lot of your time. Simply pause for a minute or two or just a few seconds. This is how you recondition your Self and how conscious choices are made, by pausing before acting. Or instead of being action oriented, maybe you have been more reactive. Your actions have been a reaction to what has been occurring in your life. Which has it been for you?

Explore your past actions to determine if you need to become more pro-active instead of re-active. Only you know, so be very honest and critical of your Self to uncover the answer.

Write down ten actions you have taken recently that were problematic. Ask your Self, "What actions have I taken in the last four months conflict with my purpose, continually contribute to the creation of problematic

The Evaluation of Self Test

situations or impedes my ability to improve a situation in my life or characteristic within my Self? Who can help me change? How long have I been taking these actions? Why do I continue to act this way? How can I change these actions? What action, if I change it today, will have the greatest impact on my Self and life immediately?'

Conditioned Responses

The next area of your BEACH is your conditioned responses. This means you have conditioned your Self to respond in basically the same way each time a particular type of situation arises. We all have them and most of us aren't even aware that this is occurring. But you must become conscious of these conditioned responses whenever they occur in order to change them.

This will give you an opportunity to pause and consider a different way to respond and act that may be more appropriate in the moment. This is when a conscious choice can be made. Also, consider what may be triggering the response; it could be a deeply rooted belief, a common location, a person, place, or thing.

For example, you get into an argument or heated discussion with your spouse and your conditioned response is to hold a grudge for a week or more, every time. Using this same example, the husband may have a conditioned response to drink or gamble after every argument. The wife may always respond by going shopping and spending money she doesn't have.

You may have a conditioned response where anytime you are depressed or severely disappointed you overeat or

Understanding Your Life Situations Part One

overindulge in something unhealthy physically or mentally. You may also have a conditioned response to argue any time someone disagrees with your point of view instead of seeing it as it is: simply another point of view.

Or, every time your supervisor asks for a volunteer to assist on a project, you avoid eye contact to avoid being asked. You may be afraid you are not smart enough or will fail. Your response is to always avoid an opportunity to explore more challenging projects. Give some consideration to some of the following questions as they may relate to you to find any conditioned responses you may need to change.

Does your daily commute to and from work bring forth any conditioned responses that are projected toward your fellow drivers? Are you continually surrounded by the same group of people? Have you taken on a role in a group and can't seem to break out of the comfort zone of choices you always make to "fit in"? What is causing you to respond the same way every time? Is it fear, guilt, anger, frustration, stress, assumptions, or laziness? Is it based on your refusal to change something about your Self or the situation at hand?

Do you respond the same way to divert attention away from a problematic situation? Why is it that you never pause to consider if there is another way to respond to the situation to change it, especially if the situation has always been problematic? What can you do to change this? How can you respond differently?

One way to respond differently is to first, make a conscious choice to respond differently. Once this conscious choice is made it will bring your awareness into

The Evaluation of Self Test

the situations where your conditioned responses happen the most. And once you become aware of how you are responding, you can start the process of changing your conditioning. Your awareness enables you to pause for a moment to consider another way to respond that is more in alignment with your purpose.

Do you have any conditioned responses that need to change? Do you have any conditioned responses that are contributing to a problematic situation? Search your matters of major importance in all the categories of your life situations for any conditioned responses that need to change. Write down your top ten conditioned responses, what you think triggers them and how you will respond differently.

Ask your Self, "What conditioned responses conflict with my purpose, continually contributes to the creation or continuance of problematic situations or impedes my ability to improve a situation in my life or characteristic within my Self? Who triggers these responses most of the time? How can I respond differently? What conditioned response, if I change it today, will have the greatest impact on my Self and life immediately?'

Habits

The last area of your BEACH is your habits. Habits are one of the biggest contributors to problematic life situations. A habit is an unconscious pattern of behavior that becomes ingrained within your Self by repetition. Habits often have triggers that activate the pattern of behavior without even knowing it. Habits are also hard to

Understanding Your Life Situations Part One

change. But you can dramatically change any situation in your life if you can change an ingrained pattern of behavior within your Self.

In addition, habits that you may consider to be positive can also have a negative effect on a life situation. It all depends on your point of view. For example: reading every day can be considered a good habit but if reading is taking away from the time you could be spending with your spouse, children, doing yard work or other household chores, it could lead to a negative situation.

Or, the habit of watching television every evening after you get home from work to relax could be keeping you from any number of other activities you say you want to do or need to do but never seem to have enough time to do.

Some other examples of common habits are procrastination, smoking, drinking alcohol, overeating, gossiping, nail biting, oversleeping, drug use (prescription and non-prescription), credit card use and abuse, exaggerating the truth, and blaming others.

Others could be arriving at work/appointments late, buying the same products from the same store, driving to and from work the same way every day when alternate routes are available, eating the same foods week after week, or vacationing in the same locations every year.

Search your matters of major importance in all the categories of your life situations for habitual behavior. Write down what you consider are your top ten positive habits and the top ten negative habits. Looking at this list, determine what are some new habits you want to start and what are some old habits you would like to end.

The Evaluation of Self Test

Again, a habit is hard to change. A repetitious pattern of behavior created it and a repetitious pattern of behavior for some period of time is the only way to change or stop it. You may even have to start a new habit in order to end an old one. Otherwise, you may feel as if there is a void in your life, some level of emptiness that is going unfulfilled.

Ask your Self, "What habits conflict with my purpose, continually contributes to the creation of problematic situations or impedes my ability to improve a situation in my life or characteristic within my Self? Who is enabling my habits? Who/what is triggering my habits? When did these habits begin? What habits do I need to change or stop? Why? What is preventing me from changing these habits? How can I change these habits? Who can help me? What habit, if I stop it today, will have the greatest impact on my Self and life immediately?"

Now that you have explored and evaluated all of the areas of your BEACH, how each of the five areas impacts each category of your life situation and the matters of major importance within them, in writing, you can move forward.

You now have a point of reference for change. With the wealth of knowledge you now possess, you should be able to easily recognize the many positive and negative influences in your life.

You can now recondition your Self by establishing new beliefs, changing environments and taking proactive, decisive action on the conscious choices you are now making. And now that you are more aware of them, be more mindful of your conditioned responses and habits and their triggers.

Understanding Your Life Situations Part One

Relax.

Smile.

Complete the prerequisite before continuing to the next chapter.

Chapter Four

Understanding Your Life Situations Part Two

Making the Choice to Change

This is the time for change, a time for action, for transformation. When you begin the process of reconditioning your Self, you will address the most immediate matters of major importance within your Self and your life situations. You will eliminate, one by one, anything that is in conflict with your purpose, creates or contributes to a problematic life situation, or impedes your ability to improve/change a situation in your life or characteristic within your Self.

Affirm in your mind right now that you have made the choice to change one area of your BEACH or another area of your life that you consider problematic today. Remove everything that has a negative influence on your life and add more positive influences. These influences could be people, places, or material things.

Make changes incrementally if they cannot be made immediately. These increments could be day by day, week by week and if necessary, year by year. Don't put too much pressure on your Self to make changes too fast though. Incremental changes are fine as long as you remain consistent and persistent in your choices.

If necessary, start by taking control of "matters of minor importance". There are a lot of people that pass the

Understanding Your Life Situations Part Two

responsibility of making choices for matters of minor importance to someone else — things like what to eat, what movie to see, which way to drive home, etc. When you are given the opportunity to choose where to go for lunch, pick a place, any place. Just begin the process of making a choice.

Don't respond by saying "it doesn't matter" or that you don't care. It does matter! If you continue to respond with, "It doesn't't matter," you are giving away your power of choice.

When you give away your power, you are the one to blame when the situation doesn't't turn out how you like. Take responsibility for your life by using your power of choice. The more you get comfortable making minor choices, the easier it will become in making choices concerning matters of major importance.

Again, if you are able to make a change in just one area of your BEACH, you will see a change in the choices you make. You will then establish a new BEACH from which you can begin the process of change again if you like. A BEACH that will allow you to get comfortable, relax and bask in the sun as your situation management skills and life situations improve.

Remember: The first aspect of your BEACH that you must choose to change is your beliefs. You must believe that you can change your Self. You must have faith that the actions you are taking are necessary to manage your life situations better. You must believe you have the power of choice in any situation. Do you believe? _____

The Evaluation of Self Test

Final Decision

Now that you have an understanding of how to recognize opportunities, weigh your options and make conscious choices, you are now ready to make your final decision. Your final decision will take all of the previous phases of situation management into consideration.

Once you make a final decision, it is important to remember that this is your best decision based on the information you had at the time. Because as time passes, the situation and information related to it may still be evolving.

Life is in a constant state of change that affects all people, places, and things. And because of this, your final decision may have to change as a result. Each combination of an opportunity, option, and choice can create different situations at different times in different aspects of your life and the lives of those closest to you. So it is necessary for you to give your final decision careful consideration, while at the same time, being mindful that some of the factors you are basing your final decision on are changing — sometimes rather dramatically.

Your final decision may be based on some action that will be taken by another person. If that person changes their mind or is suddenly unavailable, it will change the way a situation will unfold for you. Or your final decision could be based on a location that you cannot now financially afford or get to. These types of situations occur every day. This is where all of the time and conscious thought you gave the situation really helps.

Understanding Your Life Situations Part Two

By knowing all of the other options and choices available, you now have an opportunity to turn what could have become a problematic situation into something good. By keeping this in mind, you can keep the negative emotions that can arise from affecting the situation. You will be able to control and manage situations better by controlling your emotions.

Once you make the final decision there should be no regrets on your part or second guessing. The situation could have changed even if you had made a different decision. Second guessing brings doubt into the mind so it is important to always stay positive and confident in your decision making, especially if you are in a position of leadership.

Another of my favorite movies is *U-571*. It is about an officer of a naval submarine who is suddenly placed into the position of captain after a torpedo strike kills the captain of his submarine. During a scene in which he and the crew are discussing how they will get out of this mess, he tells them, "I don't know. I don't know how."

His doubt in his decision making and leadership abilities during this critical situation placed doubt in the crew as to his ability to save their lives. Later on in his cabin, the leading chief of sub reminds him that he should never say those words to his crew. That he is the leader of the ship, "the Skipper", and even if he is unsure of the best decision to make, that as the Skipper he "always knows what to do whether he does or not."

He taught him that he should always display confidence in his decisions no matter how unlikely the decision is to work out. You must display this same confidence in your

The Evaluation of Self Test

decision making. Remember: having a purpose builds confidence. It's simply a matter of making a decision and being confident about it. You must have a knowing or feeling that it is the best decision you can make at the time — right or wrong.

The key is to build confidence in your ability to make decisions, to make better decisions than you have made before through practice and repetition. And remember: you won't always have time to wait for a situation to become static or fixed. Make the best decision you can based on the information you have and move forward until the situation has changed and is more in alignment with your purpose.

Personal Example

Like most people, my life has been full of choices and decisions — some good, some great and some not so good and some, not so great. My first big decision, the kind that involved a matter of major importance, happened at the age of thirteen. I didn't know it at the time but it turned out to be a life changing decision. I was informed during middle school that I had an opportunity to attend a liberal arts high school or a vocational school.

So I had two options. One was a liberal art high school that taught classes to prepare you for the business world. It was also the designated high school for my neighborhood. The other option was a vocational school. It was further away and taught classes that provided you with a skill in a trade, classes like auto mechanics, aviation, electronics, architectural drafting, plastics, welding, etc. The concept was that the student would be able to graduate from high

Understanding Your Life Situations Part Two

school and begin working immediately in their chosen trade or at least be able to begin an apprenticeship program in their chosen field.

There were also other factors that affected my decision that I had to consider. I could go to the school where all of my friends were going or I could go to the school where everyone would be a stranger. Of course, all my friends wanted me to go to the local high school. But I felt that if they were real friends, the kind where friendships last regardless of distance or the school you attend, they would always be my friends.

Otherwise, I felt I could make new friends and at the same time, force my Self out of my comfort zone and into situations where I would have to be more vocal as well as social. I figured that is the only way to make new friends and meet people, right?

Another choice in my decision was how I was going to get to school. The liberal arts school was within walking distance, less than a mile. The vocational school was about three miles away. You could walk but if you are familiar with Chicago winters, you don't want to walk three miles at 6 AM in the morning. I would have to take the city bus.

So after building an understanding of the opportunity I had and weighing my options, it was time to make a choice between the two schools. I decided I had to think long term; get a job in my trade after high school or go to college?

So my first final decision of major importance was to attend the vocational school. After four years, I graduated with a specialty in the field of electronics. And what do you know, before I even graduated, I was offered a job that I just couldn't refuse.

The Evaluation of Self Test

Let me lay it out for you as it was laid out for me. Review this job offer and at the end decide: If you were seventeen in 1978, graduating from high school without any scholarship offers and you were offered this job, would you have taken it? And for that matter, if you were offered this job today would you take it?

Job Offer: <u>Aircraft Electrician</u> (4 year initial contract)

1. You will receive two months of familiarization training at one of three facilities of your choice upon beginning your contract.
2. The position requires that you travel a minimal amount of time at a maximum of 30 days per year.
3. You will have guaranteed advancement opportunities to salary and position.
4. You will receive annual evaluations to discuss your individual performance. These may be used to determine your eligibility for promotion.
5. You will be paid every two weeks.
6. 30 days paid vacation and unlimited sick leave with a doctor's approval.
7. All national holidays off.
8. You will have the opportunity to travel to exotic locations like Hawaii, Guam, Portugal, Philippines, and others.
9. You will be given the opportunity to volunteer for various civic and organizational programs.
10. 75% of tuition costs will be paid for by the company.
11. All medical services are free of charge.
12. Discounts on food purchases and housing costs.

Understanding Your Life Situations Part Two

13. Most business locations have a golf course, swimming pools and fitness centers, tennis courts, automotive repair shops, and various other retail and recreational facilities.
14. You are required to negotiate a new contract every three to four years. Extension requests must be made in writing. You may be required to relocate upon initiating a new contract.
15. You will receive retirement income, for life, based on the salary you were paid upon leaving the company if you remain with the company for a minimum of twenty years.

What would be your decision? For me, it was a no brainer. How could I refuse this, right? The decision to accept this job offer was the second decision of major importance I made that would provide me with the keys to success I enjoy in life today. Without even knowing it, I was practicing Situation Management.

I was presented with an opportunity; I weighed my options by brainstorming, made a conscious choice and a final decision related to a matter of major importance that changed my life situation for the better.

This was the establishment of a foundation in Situation Management that served me for twenty-one years while working for that company. And I'm still receiving all the benefits from those two decisions today. This company, in case you haven't already figured it out, was the U.S. Navy.

I established my foundation for Situation Management at an early age and it is still solid today. It doesn't matter when you start building yours as long as you start. Make a

The Evaluation of Self Test

final decision that you will start building yours today. Always be confident in your decision making abilities. You are the "Skipper" of your life situations. You are in control. You make the final decision in all matters of importance in your life.

If you make a decision and the results don't meet your expectations, look for new opportunities and new options. Make a new choice and decision until all of your expectations are met.

Don't build a foundation for situation management that can't stand the test of time. Don't build it on sand which can wash away during the storms that life situations can bring. Build it upon solid rock — on the strength and power of your conscious choices and decisions. This is the kind of foundation that will stand the tests of time, emotions, mistakes or disappointments, time after time, situation after situation.

Now that you have made the final decision to manage your life situations better, you might be thinking it's time for a break. Or maybe, you can relax for a while. Sorry but this is not the time to take a break. As I said earlier, life is changing around us faster than we can even imagine.

The forces that are at work against you are changing as rapidly as the ones that are working for you. You must stay ever vigilant and watchful for any changes that affect your Self and your life situation. This is the time for monitoring and evaluating the new situation that you created or changed by your final decision.

Understanding Your Life Situations Part Two

Monitoring and Evaluating the New Situation

Hopefully, you have taken the bull by the horns and made a conscious choice and final decision to improve your life situation to bring about some type of change in your life. This change will be different for each person. From the decision to change jobs or the city you live in, to something simpler like which way to drive to work or which clothes to wear to work. Decision making can be easy or complex. Only you know what your level of comfort is in a given situation.

But whether the decision was easy or hard, I cannot overemphasize the importance of staying engaged in the process of change by periodically monitoring and evaluating your life situations to determine if you're final decision is providing you with what it is that you are trying to achieve.

Are your decisions helping you change your Self or your life situations? Can you experience your purpose anytime you want? Are you getting from point A to B? Did a decision create problems with cross connected life situations that you did not anticipate?

Are you working harder and longer hours and it's causing you health problems? Does the time you spend at the gym, playing golf, or bowling reduce the time you spend with your family? Is your work performance suffering because you are now going to college?

Monitor and evaluate all of your matters of major importance in all of your life situation categories to ensure everything is moving in alignment with your purpose.

The Evaluation of Self Test

When I made the decision to attend a vocational school, one of my goals was to learn a trade. I achieved that. When I graduated from high school and decided to serve in the U.S. Navy, I wanted to travel, earn a good salary, secure a retirement income, meet new people, etc. I was able to achieve all of those desires as well.

Don't get me wrong though, there were a lot of challenges along the way. No one's life journey is completely perfect in all aspects. But by periodically monitoring and evaluating my life situations, I could see that I was taking advantage of the majority of the opportunities, options, and choices presented to me.

And as I look back on those decisions that related to all of my matters of importance, I made the best decision with the information I had at the time. And that's all you can do — do the best you can with what you have.

You must continually monitor how the people, places, and things involved in your decision are affected by it. Evaluate if the situation has made a change for the better or worse. Have a plan B, C, or D ready if necessary. Be as proactive and aggressive as you feel is required to achieve whatever it is you desire.

Don't let minor setbacks deter you. In some situations, it may take a bad decision or a few mistakes for you to learn the best way to manage a situation. Failure is the greatest teaching tool available to us. So focus on the positive in all decisions and resulting situations. And remember to Find An Interesting Lesson in anything you feel you "failed" at.

These are the four phases of Situation Management. Once you have learned these phases, you will have gained

Understanding Your Life Situations Part Two

the knowledge necessary to align your life situations with your purpose. You have learned how to take advantage of the opportunities available to you in order to manage your life situations more effectively. You now know that as opportunities arise, you must weigh your options and make a conscious choice as it relates to the situation.

Once you have made your choice you can resolve in your mind that you have made your final decision, with no regrets. You now know that once you make your final decision, you will then need to simply monitor the situation and evaluate it as it evolves, as it changes, to make sure it meets your expectations. If not, repeat the four phases until the situation changes to your satisfaction.

This does not guarantee that a situation will not be problematic but it will put you in control of the situation. Problems will always arise. The way in which you handle the problems will determine how long the situation lasts, its impact on your Self, and if it is necessary to take additional action after it is monitored and evaluated.

Situation Management is a cycle that never ends. You will become proficient in identifying each phase as it occurs with time and practice. Your ability to identify areas of your BEACH that may need to change will also improve.

As your life changes, your situations will change and your decisions will change to adjust to them. It is a never-ending process of learning — learning more about your Self, your likes and dislikes. But remember, the payoff is the fulfillment of your dreams and desires as you live a purposeful lifestyle.

The Evaluation of Self Test

Exercise

The purpose of this chapter is to evaluate your understanding of the many situations your life is divided into and to provide you with some techniques and ideas to help you manage them better, especially when they become problematic. It is now important for you to put these solutions to use in the day to day management of your life situations, especially those that concern matters of major importance.

This exercise will help you become more familiar with the four phases of Situation Management and enhance your awareness of the many variables involved in life situations. The more you practice stimulating your mind, the easier it will become.

To begin, select one or more situations that you observe by watching a program on TV such as a movie, drama, sitcom or the news, or it could be a situation related to social media or even someone else's situation that you are familiar with. Try to put aside any judgment, prejudices, stereotypes, or beliefs about the people, places, and things involved and evaluate the situation for what it is.

Decide what would be the best way to manage it better without anger or a high level of emotion. This is a key point to change a life situation: manage each situation as it arises, calmly, logically and with controlled emotion. Bring your purpose, your natural state into it if necessary.

As you watch the situation unfold, apply each phase of Situation Management to it. Look for some of the points you learned about in this chapter such as: Was there a lack of awareness on the part of anyone regarding what you

Understanding Your Life Situations Part Two

would consider "matters of major importance" that contributed to the situation? Did any of the characters have unrealistic expectations? What opportunities and options were missed or not taken advantage of? What are some of the choices and decisions that people made that caused or contributed to a problematic life situation? What aspects of their BEACH played a key role in how the situation improved or worsened?

What lessons can be learned from any failures you observed? Was the environment or location they were in or frequented a factor in the outcomes? What conditioned responses or habits were significant enough to warrant a change in behavior? Which final decisions that were made by each person involved had the most impact on the situation? Did this decision make the situation better or more problematic? Look for as many examples as you can find related to situation management and play around with "what if" scenarios.

For example, what if a person did not choose to do this or that? What if they had chosen to go here instead of there? What if they had asked this person instead of that one? What if she responded differently to the news? Play around with all the situations and scenarios you can think of until you can readily see all the little nuances of the different situations. Write as many answers as you can. Use the 5W1H Method of Brainstorming to evaluate the situations even deeper.

Now, here comes the hard part: Select one or more situations in each category of your life situation that is a matter of major importance and or is problematic. The situation you choose should be something that you have not

The Evaluation of Self Test

taken any action to resolve. Again, just as before, look for some of the points you learned about in this chapter.

Look at the opportunities that were available and the choices you made. Look at your BEACH to find areas that need more attention. What changes can you make? What if you changed your responses in certain situations? What action can you take now to make a situation less problematic? How can you make your life situations more peaceful, most of the time?

Now is the time to put in the work to really evaluate all of your life situations and find areas that need to be changed. This is an opportunity that you need to take advantage of. Evaluate your Self and your life situations like no one else can so that you can make conscious choices and final decisions that will have the most impact in the days ahead. This is one of the most important parts of your evaluation and test. Complete this exercise now.

Your Philosophy for a Purposeful Lifestyle

You now have the insight you need to create your philosophy. All of the information you wrote down during the evaluation of your BEACH and the previous exercise has provided you with a wealth of information and insight into your Self and the life situation you have created or are involved in.

You should now know what needs to be changed within your Self to change your life situation and also have a good idea about the principles of behavior you need to create that will help you exist with your desired purpose on a daily basis.

Understanding Your Life Situations Part Two

As stated before, your philosophy will establish the principles by which you act and behave while you exist and live with purpose. Your principles will establish the plan of action by which you change any situation in your life that is not in alignment with your purpose. It will help you overcome some of the difficulties you will encounter that push and pull at the corners of your being in the form of people, places, and things.

Your philosophy should be written out as several principle statements and it should address at least ten specific areas of your lifestyle, specific situations or specific behavioral issues that may prevent you from experiencing your purpose.

At a minimum, you should create a principle for your philosophy for these types of situations first:

1. Any situation that prevents you from existing in your natural state.
2. Any situation that you want to create or improve because it allows you to exist in or brings you close to your natural state almost immediately.
3. Any situation in any Category of Life Situations that is not in alignment with your purpose.
4. An area of your BEACH that needs to be brought into alignment with your purpose.

And remember: you want a philosophy that creates a mindset, an attitude or demeanor —a way to live and act, not a goal. For example, a principle in your philosophy could be "to live a healthy lifestyle". A healthy mind and body contribute to a healthy existence. This would be your

The Evaluation of Self Test

daily mindset. Your daily goals would be to eat better foods, exercise daily, refrain from alcohol and drug consumption, etc.

Your philosophy will then create an attitude of poise, confidence, and presence because you know what you want and you know the kind of lifestyle you want to live. Your frame of mind is centered on taking the action that is necessary to bring your purpose and philosophy into your everyday experience. This presence allows you to live more of your life in the moment of every situation.

By living in the moment, you can reduce the amount of time spent regretting the past or fearing the future. You free your mind of past errors because you become aware that they were necessary to get you where you are today. You have no fear of the future because you are directing the creative force within you to create your future with your actions and behaviors in the moment.

The following is an example of a philosophy I created for the purpose I provided in the previous chapter. Again, my purpose was to:

"Exist as a being of happiness and peace."

The principles of my philosophy were:

1. I decided to always be happy while living a lifestyle of leisure.
2. I decided to only work for charity as my way of giving back to society.
3. I decided to be decisive, consistent, and patient in all of my actions and behaviors.

Understanding Your Life Situations Part Two

4. I decided to seek to understand; to understand differences of thought to bring peace in all of my personal relationships and life situations.
5. I decided to enjoy my physical health by participating in energizing activities, eating and drinking in healthy moderation and regularly scheduling physician checkups.
6. I decided I will stimulate the natural creativity within me by reading and listening to idea-filled materials regularly.
7. I decided to manage my wealth by balancing my investments and spending to ensure my wealth lasts a lifetime.
8. I decided to take time to spend with or help family and friends.
9. I decided to remain open to new ideas and to remain flexible to change in all of my life situations.
10. I decided to be forgiving of my Self and others and to seek the good in all people and life situations.

Each principle helped me to exist with my chosen purpose. Each principle helped me remain aware of the areas that bring peace and happiness into my life. Each principle set an expectation that all will be well within my Self and my life situations if I simply follow these principles.

These principles worked for me at the time I created them. But as my life situations changed, I changed them to accommodate the changes that life presented me. Keep this in mind when you create yours. You can change them at any time. But you have to start somewhere. Create

The Evaluation of Self Test

whatever it is you feel you need to guide your Self or apply to your life situations today. Create ten or more principles that will help you exist in your natural state without even giving it a thought. This is an important evaluation point.

Create your philosophy now.

Summary

Your life situations are your life, broken down into individual situations similar to scenes in a movie or TV program. Some are happy or sad and some are comical or filled with drama. But unlike most things on TV, your life situations are real. You can't just change the channel when something happens in your life that you don't like. You have to take positive, affirmative action to change a situation.

The two chapters on Understanding Your Life Situations Part One and Two, provided you with the opportunity to pause and evaluate the situations you have created or are involved in. Do you like what you see? If not, use the ideas provided in this chapter to help you align your life situations with your purpose.

Begin by resolving all of your problematic life situations while staying mindful of the cross connected relationships related to each one. Use the four phases of situation management. Situation management helps focus your time and attention and promotes awareness of the types of situations, you are creating or involved in.

Awareness allows you to pause and consider the opportunities that are available to change your Self or the

Understanding Your Life Situations Part Two

situation. Pausing helps you weigh your options so that you can make a conscious choice as to what you want. You must be continually mindful of your mental attitudes which convey your beliefs and how they affect your choices. Your environment and the actions you take when you are there as well as the unconscious choices you make by your conditioned responses and habits must also be taken into consideration.

Make your final decision in a confident and timely manner with no regrets and stay mindful of your evolving situations as the changes you made begin to unfold. You must ensure that everything is working together in accordance with the principles contained in your philosophy. You will then be able to experience your purpose on a daily basis as your life situations move into alignment with your purpose and you live in accordance with your philosophy.

The Evaluation of Self Test

Quiz Two

Answer all of the questions on a sheet of paper or in your journal. Answer them to the best of your ability. And remember, there are no wrong answers. What you write is for your benefit.

1. Make a list of at least ten situations in your life today that you consider to be a matter of major importance. Which ones are problematic and why?
2. What is the most problematic situation in your life today?
3. What person is contributing the most to this situation and why?
4. What belief is contributing the most to this situation? Is it valid or an assumption?
5. What environment is contributing the most to this situation?
6. What conditioned responses or habits are contributing the most to this situation?
7. Why are you tolerating this situation? (if it has not been resolved within three days of first occurring)
8. What is your contribution to the situation both positive and negative?
9. What action needs to be taken and why?
10. What is your plan of action to resolve the situation or manage the situation better?
11. Did you complete your philosophy? If no, why not?
12. Did you complete the last exercise? If no, why not?

Understanding Your Life Situations Part Two

Relax.

Smile.

Complete the prerequisite before continuing to the next chapter.

Chapter Five

Understanding the Importance of Goals

Goals

We have reached the halfway mark of your evaluation and review. You should now know what your purpose is and a have written purpose statement. You should also have a great understanding of your life situations and a written philosophy. Your philosophy should have at least ten principles that will enable you to align your existing and future life situations with your purpose. Now we will evaluate and review your understanding of the importance of setting goals.

Goals and goal settings have been around for a long time. A goal is basically a singular plan of action to accomplish something. When you set a goal, you are setting a plan of action in motion with a start date and projected end date. The goals you create at the end of this chapter will be the detailed actions for the purposeful plan you established with your philosophy to change your life situations.

Unfortunately, most people are not taught the benefits of goals or how to create them until they are in college or work for a large company that encourages their use. I feel that a course on the topic of goals should be taught at every level of education from elementary school through college.

Understanding The Importance of Goals

At some point in everyone's life, a thought or vision for the future is formed in their minds. It could be to accomplish something such as becoming a cheerleader, getting straight A's in school, starting a new career, getting a college degree, winning an athletic medal or championship, losing weight, learning a new skill or becoming debt free to name a few.

Some people are successful in accomplishing these goals but for most, as time passes, so does the thought and vision. It fades away, like a dream when you wake up. And unfortunately, these could be some of the most impactful actions a person can take to enhance or change their life situations.

I have found, during my life experiences, that there are two main reasons that these thoughts and visions fade away. The first reason is that they are never written down. By simply writing down your thought or vision for the future, the action necessary to complete a goal is set in motion. By simply putting pen to paper (or your fingers on a keyboard) you will make a mental commitment to the completion of your goal.

Once it is written down, you can visually implant the thought in your mind. By writing it down, you can see it on a regular basis and affirm it aloud if necessary. Once your dream for the future is written down, you can clarify the details of what it is you have decided. This can serve to help clear any doubt, fear, or anxiety as to whether or not your goal can be accomplished.

A goal that is thought about, visualized, written about, and verbally affirmed has a far better chance of being completed than one that is simply thought about.

The Evaluation of Self Test

The second reason why the visions, thoughts, and dreams of so many people go unfulfilled is that they are unwilling to take the time. This is a part of your test: to determine if you will take the time necessary to sit down, write out the details of what you want, and then create written goals to accomplish it.

I don't have time, I can't take the time, it takes too much time, how long will it take and it takes too long are some of the thoughts that replace the vision and dreams. The amazing fact is that we all have time to do whatever we want to do, believe we can do, are willing to do or are forced to do, whether we feel like it or not. Time isn't the issue. Everyone has 24 hours in a day. What you do with that time is your choice.

Ask your Self, "What else am I doing that is taking up so much of my time?" You take time to watch TV, browse through post after post on social media, and take picture after picture to post your own Selfies. You have time during lunch breaks that could be used more productively and time that you spend doing other mindless tasks that can be reduced or eliminated. Time can be found. Any person that wants to can find at least an hour of their day to commit to a goal they want to achieve.

But unfortunately during these times of "I want it here and now", many people are unwilling to wait or be patient enough to take the time required for the plan to unfold — for the pieces of the puzzle to come together. One setback is enough to bring their vision to an end. It then becomes something to talk about during idle conversation like I was going to, I always wanted to, I tried to but he, she, they wouldn't help me, it was too hard, too time consuming, etc.

Understanding The Importance of Goals

Excuse after excuse becomes their justification for doing nothing.

But this will not happen to you. That's because you now know the advantages of writing down your goals. You now know you must manage your time better. You now know you must take the time that is required, no matter how small the increment, in order to bring your visions, thoughts, and dreams to life through the achievement of your goals.

Benefits of Goals

Goals are beneficial to you in many ways. Goals facilitate change. Goals pull you out of the comfort zone of living life randomly. Goals direct the focus of your attention. Goals change your perspective on life. Goals provide a way for you to evaluate and measure where you were to where you are. Goals motivate, stimulate, and get you moving, talking, interacting, and learning while overcoming fears and obstacles.

The following are just a few more important examples of what goals can provide. You can easily remember how goals can help you by using the letters in its spelling.

<u>Goals provide a:</u>

Good
Opportunity to
Analyze your
Life
Situation

The Evaluation of Self Test

The process of change begins when you analyze your life situations to determine where a change will be the most beneficial to you. This is why it was so important for you to complete a thorough analysis of your life situations in the previous chapter. Now that the analysis is complete, it is the perfect opportunity to create goals.

No matter what your life situation is whether good or bad, you should periodically take an assessment of where you have been, where you are at the present moment and where you are headed. If you do not know this information, you are truly living your life as Jim Rohn describes as a "wandering generality". This means that you choose to live without a specific direction, that you are mostly reactive instead of proactive, that you respond to life as it happens to you rather than choosing to make things happen "on purpose".

Goals provide the opportunity to review what is meaningful to you. It is a good opportunity to ask your Self the questions needed to get you on the road to success in fulfilling your purpose and dreams. Questions like: What distractions have I allowed to turn my focus, my attention away from my purpose? What is the state of my life situation? What goals can I create to change this? How can I improve my chances to get a new job or a better paying job? Are my finances in order? What is the state of my mental and physical health? What have I allowed my Self to become addicted to? What habits do I need to stop and what habits can I start?

Goals also provide a good opportunity to take an assessment of all of your personal and professional relationships. Ask your Self: Is it time to create goals to

Understanding The Importance of Goals

establish a new network of friends, end some old relationships, or simply change some aspect of a relationship for the better? Are these relationships having a positive or negative impact on my life situation?

You should make it a habit to pause on a regular basis from your day to day activities to analyze your life situation to see where a goal can have the greatest impact. Then, take the time to write down your goals and take action as soon as possible.

<u>Goals help you:</u>

Go
On
After
Losing
Something

The loss of someone or something special to you can be emotionally and mentally hard to move forward from. The loss of a family member, close friend or co-worker, a job, money, a home, marriage or physical/mental abilities can be devastating for some people. Even the loss of a family pet can bring about the same type of grief. But no matter what it is, the ability to go on after the loss can take days, months and/or years to overcome.

Thoughts related to the loss can invade your mind to the point that it disrupts your ability to sleep. These situations can also bring doubt, guilt, and fear to the forefront of our minds. We continue to ask ourselves: Why did this happen? What did I do wrong to make this happen? What could I have done differently? What will happen to me if it

The Evaluation of Self Test

happens again? It's all my fault... if I had only done this or that. These repetitious questions and thoughts in the mind can lead to numerous negative emotions if they are not brought to an end.

I have personally experienced several of these losses. I have lost two jobs, a home, a marriage, and my father. Each one affected me with different levels of grief. After each loss, I had to accept the fact that nothing lasts forever. It is the natural cycle of life. People and things will come in and out of our lives throughout our lifetime and our life situations will be affected by this continual change as a result.

The good thing to remember is that the emotional impact the loss has on your life will slowly fade away with time. But with every loss, a void within your Self and your life may continue to exist. What is needed is something to fill the void. This is where goals help you go on after the loss.

Goals fill the void. They occupy your thoughts to distract you from what's missing and from the emotional pain you may experience. By setting goals, I was able to acquire a new job, a new home, and wife and to accept the fact that my father had passed on just as we all will. Goals definitely helped me go on after each loss.

Goals help you get back on the road to recovery. Just as a flat tire leaves you stranded on the side of the road, the loss of something or someone can leave you stranded in your life until the grieving is over or the void is filled. But goals act as the "fix-a-flat" that gets you back on the path to your purpose, to the fulfillment of your dreams and

Understanding The Importance of Goals

aspirations. They help you to continue the journey you were on before the loss.

Goals provide the action steps you need to slowly begin again, to reengage your Self in whatever is necessary to move forward. The goal can focus on creating a memorial for the loss of loved ones, writing a new resume for your next job or career, making plans to build or buy a new home, creating a budget to get your finances in order, as well as researching the latest in technological advances to help you overcome any physical limitations you now have.

There are also plenty of children that need adopting as well as pets in shelters that need a new home. And if the loss was your faith in God or life itself, setting a goal to reestablish your relationship with God through nightly prayer, seeking out a church/spiritual leader to assist or the giving of one's Self through Self-sacrifice/service can get you back on the road to recovery. If you find your Self asking God, "why me," one of God's answers lies in the setting of goals to guide you so you can help your Self.

Another point to remember is that as you change your Self and your life situations, you should be prepared to lose more things. As you change, the relationships you have with some people will change. Some will change with you while others will resist the change. As a result of this, you will find that you no longer need certain people in your life. In addition, you will lose interest in the need to have certain material things or the need to go to certain places again.

But these types of losses are the kind that will help you move toward what you want even faster. These losses will be like dropping the dead weight that you never even realized was there. As these losses accumulate, it will

The Evaluation of Self Test

become easier to deal with any future losses that may not be as pleasant. Each loss will make you stronger and establish a foundation for faster recovery from a more heartfelt loss. And this can be accomplished by setting goals.

<u>Goals allow the:</u>

Gifts
Of
All
Living
Spirits to Manifest into Reality

Everyone is born with God given talents but some of us never take advantage of them or share them with the rest of humanity. The bible says in Romans 12-6, 7, 8; "God has given each of us the ability to do certain things well. So if God has given you the ability of prophesy, speak out when God is speaking through you. If your gift is that of serving others, serve them well. If you are a teacher, do a good job of teaching. If your gift is to encourage others, do it joyfully. If you have money, share it generously. If God has given you leadership ability, take the responsibility seriously. And if you have the gift of showing kindness to others, do it gladly."

Some Christian churches have given names to these gifts such as exhorter, giver, teacher, etc. So while each of us has a gift, why is it that we don't use them? My feeling is that some gifts can manifest easily for some but take time and effort for others. Setting goals to develop your gift to

Understanding The Importance of Goals

its fullest allows them to manifest into reality faster than they would without setting goals. You may have a wonderful voice made for singing but without a concentrated effort toward its development, it may never be heard by another.

During my childhood and early adulthood, I was often told I was shy and too quiet — that I should speak up so others could hear me. I just figured it was my nature to be quiet. But I always felt I had a gift for speaking, teaching, and even leading others. I then decided to develop the gifts I felt I had by setting goals in each area.

I enrolled in teaching and facilitator courses of instruction. I also completed public speaking classes and group oriented courses in leadership and team building to refine my gifts. Soon after, I was able to share my gifts with hundreds of people by teaching and facilitating classes and leading/guiding others in their personal growth and development in the workplace and their lives.

So what is your gift? What do you have a natural ability to do? What comes so easy to you that you don't even have to think about it? Or, what is the thought that continually comes to your mind that you want to do but never have? What job do you want or what business would you like to start but never had enough courage to pursue? What is holding you back? This may be the gift that you were born with that has been left in its infancy, one that's never had a chance to grow.

It all starts with a vision — seeing your Self livings your gift and actively using it. If you can see it, can imagine it being a reality, it can happen. The American philosopher, William James said, "There is a law in

The Evaluation of Self Test

psychology that if you form a picture in your mind of what you would like to be, and you keep and hold that picture there long enough, you will soon become exactly as you have been thinking."

All you need to do is set some goals. Put pen to paper and write out all of the things you need to do to make it happen. Write as much detail as you can think of. If you need to do some research first, make that a goal. If there are numerous people you need to contact, make that a goal.

To move from infancy you have to crawl before you can walk and walk before you can run. Be patient and slowly begin the process of completing one goal after the other until you achieve your ultimate goal and purpose.

Goals can manifest all of your dreams into reality if you have faith and believe in them strong enough and long enough. As Les Brown said, "If you set goals and go after them with all the determination you can muster, your gifts will take you places that will amaze you." As you move toward growing your gifts, you will become even more energized as you see your Self getting closer and closer to your goal. The people you interact with may also become inspired to work on their gifts.

As your joy and enthusiasm increases, there will be others with the same aspirations that may get caught up in your whirlwind of success. You will amaze your Self at how energized you become as your gifts manifest into reality.

Understanding The Importance of Goals

Goals Create Expectations

And finally, goals create expectations. Goals create an expectation of achievement or success whether they are created for an individual or business. Every organization I have ever been associated with had expectations. Their expectations can be seen in several aspects of the business' plan to achieve success.

They were written in the form of a mission statement that described the purpose of the business, outlined into goals to document how they would achieve their purpose, and compiled into a step by step plan of actions or objectives to accomplish their goals. And, the business had an expectation that everyone associated with it would perform at a certain level in order to achieve the business' plan, purpose, and goals.

Your plan of action will create the same type of expectations in your personal life. By creating a plan of action, you will create the expectation that your purpose, philosophy, and goals can be achieved. Everything you have read to this point in the book should have created an expectation that you can do whatever it is you decide to do when you want to do it.

You should already have an expectation that you can change and bring order into your life situations. You should already have an expectation that you can and will live a life with purpose. You should already have an expectation that obstacles will sometimes stand in your way and at the same time, expect that you can overcome them using all of the resources that are available to you.

The Evaluation of Self Test

And when you complete this chapter, you should have an expectation that everyone and everything will work together, no matter how bad the situation may seem at the time, toward the completion of your goals. Remember: every situation you find your Self in can be of value toward the completion of your goals — you simply have to look for it.

As you work toward the completion of your goals, you will come to expect more of your Self and others. You should expect more because you are now working from a different point of reference, a new BEACH and a purpose for your life. You will no longer settle for substandard performance or behavior. You will no longer settle for anything provided from others to be less than what you would expect if you had done it your Self.

As you incrementally move closer and closer toward the completion of your goals, your level of energy and enthusiasm will incrementally build. Your anticipation of obtaining that which you desire will grow with every step you take during your journey.

When you have a goal, it's like having a winning lottery ticket in your hand. As each correct number is read off, your anticipation of winning the jackpot builds with an undeniable adrenaline rush. You can experience this same type of feeling when you progress toward and complete your goals. The completion of your goals will be your own, personal jackpot of success and gratification.

Understanding The Importance of Goals

Unexpected Outcomes

Another point to keep in mind is that sometimes a goal will lead you to an outcome that is totally unexpected. As the great martial artist, Bruce Lee, said, "A goal is not always meant to be reached; it often serves as something to aim at." Jim Rohn also expressed, "Be careful what you become in the pursuit of your goals." The journey you take to reach your goals will surely change parts of you along the way and at its completion. Stay mindful of these changes no matter how small.

You may need to reevaluate your desires if the outcome at the completion of your goal is not what you expected. As your desires change, your goals may need to change along with them. Don't become so single minded in purpose toward the completion of your goals that you lose sight of what's happening in the present moment.

The journey to the completion of your goals should be as satisfying as actually reaching the goal because you are actively engaged in an activity YOU have chosen. There will be all types of challenges along the way in the form of people, places, and things. You should still enjoy your journey as much as you can in spite of this. Be accepting of the pain as well as the pleasure of it all.

And if for some reason you don't reach your goal, don't quit. Rethink your plan and create a new goal; a goal that creates new expectations of achievement, success, and performance, one that captures your attention and satisfies you mentally, physically, spiritually, and emotionally.

The Evaluation of Self Test

Creating Your Measurable Action Plan (MAP)

> Pablo Picasso stated, *"Our goals can only be reached through the vehicle of a plan, in which we must fervently believe, and upon which we must vigorously act. There is no other route to success."*

Now that you know some of the benefits of goals and what they can do for you, it's time to learn how to go about creating them. Before any new project or task is undertaken, it is best to create a plan that provides the directions on how to accomplish it. This project could be to learn a new skill, build something, or even take a trip in a car.

No matter what it is, it is best to have a plan before you begin. This "plan" isn't just something that is thought about and then started without some detailed thought. This plan must be in writing. Without a written commitment to the plan, one or several steps can be missed or forgotten along the way.

If a new home is being built there is a written construction plan. When starting a new business there is a written business plan. If you are learning to play an instrument or taking a course in school, there is a lesson plan. When you are taking a long trip in a car, you can get a plan from a Global Positioning System (GPS). You simply enter the destination address into your car GPS.

The GPS will provide you with an electronically-mapped out plan to get you to your destination. The GPS will direct you when to turn left or right and when you are over the speed limit. It can tell you what road you are on,

Understanding The Importance of Goals

the next road to take, alternate routes, how far you have traveled and the approximate time of your arrival. It can also provide information concerning obstacles on the road such as accidents, construction, and other traffic delays that may be on the road ahead of you.

The plan you create will provide similar information for you. It can be as detailed as you decide. It will be your plan of action that takes you to a destination of your choosing in a timeframe that works best for you. The name of the plan that you will create to reach your destination is called a Measurable Action Plan, a MAP.

This MAP will serve as your plan of action in the form of written goals. Your MAP will help you reach your destinations and complete your goals faster and easier than if you did not have it. Your MAP will be for your personal benefit. Others may reap some of the benefits of your plan but this MAP is for your primary use.

It is said that plans are meant to be broken. Construction plans are changed daily to account for unforeseen issues during the building process. Business plans are dramatically changed before the first customer walks through the door. GPS mapping is updated on almost a daily basis.

Your MAP is yours to revise, edit, or rewrite at any time as well. Your first MAP will contain all of the goals you choose today, at this current stage of your life. As time passes and your situations begin to change, you may have new goals and desires that you want to pursue. Your situations and priorities may change if you get married, become a parent, inherit or win a large sum of money, your health improves or declines and so on.

The Evaluation of Self Test

Use a copy of your original MAP to adjust to these situational changes. This will be your working copy. Your working copy will allow you to capture these changes in the form of new goals and new priorities. But always keep your original MAP. This will serve as a reference point so you will always know where you started your journey. You can then measure your progress from one point in time to another during times of reflection and periods of transition.

Please keep this point in mind though: if you find your Self making numerous changes to your working copy in a relatively short period of time, you may need to stop and pause for a little while. This delay will give you the opportunity to reconsider what your true goals really are. Take this time to determine where you really want to go and what you really want for your Self.

This is the time to ensure your goals are in alignment with your purpose and the philosophy for the lifestyle you have decided to live. You should also ensure your goals are addressing any problematic life situations you have created or allowed your Self to become involved in.

You may also need to ask for help in deciding the best path to take. Don't be afraid to ask for help from those that will tell you the truth. You may have gotten lost, lost from all of the changes that have occurred and, as a result, you made a wrong turn somewhere. Too many changes may indicate a need to start from the beginning and create a new MAP. Don't hesitate to create a new MAP and start out refreshed and renewed.

Understanding The Importance of Goals

Three Types of Goals

There are three types of goals you will use to create your MAP. They are long term goals, short term goals, and incremental goals.

Long term goals are those that will be achieved in a period of a year or more. Most of these types of goals will be completed in one to five years but can extend to whatever period you choose. A word of caution though: goals created for periods longer than five years should not be considered when you first start out.

Long term goals require a lot of thought and careful planning to complete. As a beginner on your journey of change, this can be a daunting task. It will be more beneficial for you to start with the next type of goal.

Short term goals are those that can be completed in one to twelve months. Focus on creating short term goals first. Focus on goals that create the biggest change in your Self and your life in the shortest amount of time. The choice is completely yours as to the goals you create. It is your MAP and it benefits you and you alone.

The last type of goal is incremental goals. Incremental goals are the key to your ability to complete your short and long term goals. Incremental goals are the key to your ability to change. Incremental goals are the goals that you will complete daily that will move you, little by little, toward the change you desire. They are your daily "things to do" that keep you focused on your short and long term goals. They promote daily focus and purposeful actions to get your Self or your life situations in right order.

The Evaluation of Self Test

When you set your plan of action in motion, you initially want to build up the experience of completing as many goals as you can as soon as possible. This has the advantage of building up your confidence — confidence in knowing "I can do it, I did it before and I can do it again!" You will build Self-confidence in your ability to accomplish whatever you desire when you see the completion of numerous incremental goals and begin enjoying the benefits of your efforts.

This will have the added benefit of helping you gain momentum — momentum that will be hard to stop. You will become motivated to take on even larger, more challenging goals. The completion of one goal will serve as the building block to achieving the next one, then the next one and so on.

Each of the three goals can be used together when the goal is large. You can use incremental goals to break down your short term goals and use short term goals to break down your long term goals.

For example, suppose your long term goal is to complete a Bachelor's degree in Economics by taking classes in the evening at the University of Big City and graduating with honors in less than 4 years. You are married with children and have a full-time job. The degree program may have a requirement of completing 100 hours of course study to complete the program.

The only way you can do this is to complete one to three classes at a time, one quarter at a time, one year at a time. You may not be able to complete this goal in 4 years considering all that is going on in your life situation at the time.

Understanding The Importance of Goals

It took over ten years for me to complete my degree by taking classes in the evening. There were some quarters when I couldn't attend college because of family or work conflicts. There were quarters when I could only take one class or none at all because of financial issues or class availability. Your situation could be similar.

But by setting a short term goal each quarter to complete one course a quarter with a "B" average or better, you can work toward the completion of your long term goal of completing your degree program and graduating with honors. You will know if the timeframe for completing the degree needs to be adjusted if you miss a quarter or two. You will also know if you need to double or triple up on classes when they are available so you can meet your long term goal. And by setting an incremental goal of nightly study, you will stay focused on your long term goal of completing your degree no matter how long it takes.

This also can be applied to losing weight. Your long term goal may be to lose 33 pounds in a year. Your short term goal could be to lose 3 pounds a month. And your incremental goal could be to exercise daily and always take the stairs instead of using the elevator. You can apply the three goals in any manner in almost any situation to achieve whatever you want.

Objectives

You should always pause before adding a goal to your MAP. You do not want to add a goal with any amount of uncertainty in your mind. An objective will allow you to

The Evaluation of Self Test

pause for a few minutes, hours, or days before you decide upon a goal.

With this in mind, you should have one or more objectives in mind when you create your goals. Objectives help ensure the reason that you are creating the goal is clear and that you have a complete understanding of what is necessary to accomplish it. Objectives clarify the importance of the goal within your Self as to why it must be completed and why you are taking the time to do it.

Write out your goal, read it over, pause and determine your objectives. You can ask your Self the 5W1H questions to generate ideas and answers. Brainstorming is one of the best ways to help determine your objectives as well as examine all aspects of the goal itself.

Objectives help answer questions like, "What is the purpose of this goal? What life situation does this goal apply to? How will this goal change my current situation? Why am I creating this goal? What am I trying to accomplish by doing this? Is this goal realistic?"

What would be some of your objectives if you were to use the previous example of completing a Bachelor's Degree in Economics? The objectives you select should help you refocus your mind when you are two years into your degree program and negative thoughts begin to cloud your mind with questions or doubt.

Thoughts like "this is too hard, why am I doing this, you know you can't finish this, it's not worth it, it's causing friction in my marriage, causing problems at work, I'm not getting enough sleep, it's taking up too much time, I might as well give up, I'm not good enough or smart enough" so on and so forth.

Understanding The Importance of Goals

Your objectives will help keep you motivated and focused if you lose the momentum you initially had when you wrote down your goal.

Measurable Actions

Now that you know the three different types of goals and the importance of objectives we will focus on the most important aspect of your MAP: your actions. Your MAP is worthless if you do not take action on the goals you create. You must take action daily in order to change any situation, especially those that are problematic.

Daily, purposeful action will bring about the greatest amount of change in your life situations. This is why it is extremely important that your actions are measurable. You can easily determine if your plan of action is effective and track your progress when it is measurable or quantified. This will enable you to document, monitor, or track your progress toward the completion of the goal.

The measures you choose depend on the goals you create. Your measure could be to track the amount of money you save or spend daily, the amount of sales you close in a month, the amount of time you spend with family or friends in a day, the amount of weight you lose in a week, the grade point average you accumulate in a year or the number of miles you run in a week.

Some other areas could be the number of alcoholic drinks you consume in a week, the number of cigarettes you smoke a day, or the number of books you read in a month. The choice is yours.

The Evaluation of Self Test

Remember, your goals are the actions you have decided to take that will change or improve some aspect of your Self or your life situation. You will only know if you are making progress if you can measure the change over a period of time. That time will be measured from the day you create the goal. This will be your starting point, your baseline, and your point of reference.

At the beginning of this book, I discussed the purpose of tests. I stated that tests evaluate something to see where it stands today — not tomorrow, now, at this moment in time. Tomorrow's results could be different. Tests give us a point of reference, a standard that we can use to determine if some type of correction or change is needed, today.

The day you create your goal and set a time/date of completion, you have decided to test your Self. You are testing your Self to see if you can do it. You are challenging your Self to determine if you have the sense of purpose, the focus and desire to achieve something you think you want so badly that you are willing to take the time required and put in the necessary effort to overcome whatever obstacle falls in your path.

Your time based, measurable goals will allow you to determine if your incremental, short term or long term goals can be reached in the timeframe you choose. Pause and find out what the cause of the delay is if you can't reach your goal in the given time. You can then determine what type of corrective action or change is required. If your goal is to lose fifty pounds in a year which amounts to about a pound a week and you have not lost a pound in two weeks, you will know in an instant that a change needs to be made.

Understanding The Importance of Goals

This pause also provides an opportunity to make a choice and decision to begin again, to reengage. To make an attitude adjustment, to determine if the goal was realistically achievable from the start considering everything that was occurring in all of your cross connected life situations. Time based measurable goals will help you find the source of any delays so you can regain any lost momentum and begin again.

Add Goals to Your MAP

We have reached another challenging part of the test — making a choice, the choice of what areas of your Self and life you want to change. We started your evaluation and review by first, selecting a purpose for your Self, second, evaluating your life situations and third, creating a philosophy to change your mindset, your approach to your life situations.

Now you must put what you have learned to practical use. This is an important evaluation point. You must now choose and decide which goals you will add to your MAP. You may have already decided on the areas you want to change as we have progressed to this point in the book. For you, the challenging part is over. You simply need to write out your goals and add them to your MAP. If you have not, here is your solution.

Create goals that help you experience your purpose or exist in your natural state every day. Create goals that allow you to experience one or all of the principles listed in your philosophy. And, create goals that will resolve a problematic life situation or, make a good situation even

The Evaluation of Self Test

better. Ask your Self, "What goal can I create will have the greatest impact on my Self or my life?"

Or start with the one thing you need the most improvement in, the one thing you complain about the most. Moreover, you can write a goal that at this moment you feel will bring peace and happiness into your life immediately. Additionally, you can create a goal that will help you overcome your biggest fear or least desirable emotion. These are all examples to help you get started.

Depending on what you decide, you may only need to add one goal to your MAP at this time. This one goal may consist of so many incremental goals that it will dominate the majority of your available time. Don't overwhelm your Self with too much at once. As I said earlier, it may be best to start with short term goals first. As you gain confidence in your ability to complete your goals, add more.

You can also use is the 5W1H Method of Brainstorming we discussed earlier. They will help you explore as many aspects of your life as possible to find areas that may need a goal created to change them. The 5W1H questions will also help ensure you have given your goals the thought and consideration necessary to bring about the change you desire. Some examples of their use are listed below.

1. Who — is contributing to a problematic situation in my life? Who else is involved? Who can help? Who can I contact?
2. What — situation, person, place or thing in my life is the most problematic? What do I want to accomplish? What do I want to change? What does

Understanding The Importance of Goals

this conflict with? What else can I do? Where — will this action be taken? Where is the best location to accomplish this? Where can I go for assistance? Where else can I go? Where should I stop/start going?
3. When — is the action starting and ending? When is enough, enough?
4. Why — am I taking this action? Why is it important? Why am I allowing this situation to continue?
5. How — will this goal be measured? How can I track my progress? How can I prevent this from happening again? How can I respond differently?

The examples listed above are just a few of the questions you could ask your Self. Asking your Self these and similar questions will help you discover what you want to change, so you can set a goal to change it. It is also a great way to determine the numerous action steps that must be completed before you can complete your long term, short term, or incremental goal.

The 5W1H method helps you create a vision. It allows you to clearly envision what it is you want to accomplish *before* you add the goal to your MAP. After using the 5W1H method over a period of time it will become even easier to create goals.

Once you have decided on one or more goals, add them to your MAP. Break your large goals down into smaller chunks by using short term goals. Break your short term goals down to even smaller chunks with incremental goals. Write your objectives below each goal as a visible reminder

The Evaluation of Self Test

of why you created it. And ensure you add a method to measure your progress toward the completion of your goal. Your actions must be measurable so you can easily see the progress (or lack thereof) you are making.

The level of detail that is added to your MAP, just like your 5W1H questions, is entirely up to you. Again, these are your goals and it is your MAP. Add as much information and detail as you feel is necessary. But be careful that you don't create a MAP with so many goals, with so much detail that you get confused and can't even follow it. It could ultimately lead you to decide that goals are too hard and aren't worth all the time and trouble it takes to follow them. Remember: Keep it simple!

Once the challenging part of adding goals to your MAP is over, take action on the most challenging aspects of your goals first. Overcome any fear or apprehension that enters your mind with a simple smile of acknowledgment and the thought, "not this time." Keep your objectives in mind and don't let anyone discourage you.

Besides your Self, peer pressure or the opinions of others may be the only other obstacle you have to overcome. Push through any negative comments and move forward. Surround your Self with people that encourage your efforts. Remember, you may need to find new people, places, and things if the old ones do not encourage you or help you achieve your goals. They may be a part of a problematic situation you are trying to change.

As Jim Rohn says, you may only want to share your "give up goals" with people, not your "go up" goals. For example, give up goals are when you decide to give up television, alcohol, gambling, smoking, or gossiping. Go up

Understanding The Importance of Goals

goals are when you decide to get a degree, get a new, higher paying job, relocate, or invest your money. Don't let the failures of other people discourage you.

I remember when I made the decision to enter the Navy at age seventeen. Everyone asked me why I would enter the Navy when everyone else was going into the Army. Ninety percent of what was said to me was what I considered negative. But I dismissed all of the negative talk. I knew what I wanted. I had set a goal and I wasn't going to let the naysayers move me from it.

And there is one more reason you may not want to share all of your goals with everyone. There may be some people in your life that will discourage you from setting goals and making changes because it will cause a change in their life. This is especially true for the people that you interact with daily or that you have a close personal relationship with.

They will resist the change because they may be forced out of their comfort zone. They may be forced to look in the mirror where they will realize they are living stagnantly. And some people will do anything to resist change, even to the point of argument. You will then have to decide if you are willing to compromise your dreams to remain with them — you will then have to decide what is more important, the achievement of your goal or your relationship with the person.

Summary

We exist in a creative universe. This is a creative world. Everywhere you look, there is creation, there is life. Setting

The Evaluation of Self Test

goals is a creative process that you can use to create the kind of lifestyle you want to live in this creative world. Setting goals is a creative process that you can use to activate the creativity within your mind.

They serve to create new ideas that can change any aspect of your Self or any situation in your life. Goals facilitate the process of change. They create new situations, get you involved in different situations and remove you from or resolve problematic situations.

Goals help you live a more purposeful life — a purposeful life of your own choosing. They help you manage all of your life situations and create new patterns of behavior that are beneficial to your Self and your life. But none of this can be accomplished if you *don't take the time to write them down*!

Writing them down provides you with the MAP you will need as you travel down the road of life and for one reason or another, you begin to lose your way. You can easily lose your focus as situation after situation arises that distracts you and moves your attention away from your incremental, short term as well as your long term goals.

It doesn't matter if you are trying to analyze your life situation, go on after losing something, or just discover your God given talents, setting goals can help you achieve your desires faster and easier than if you didn't set them. This has been proven time and time again. All you have to do is decide what you want to do.

Start by creating the vision of your goal in your mind. See your goal with your mind's eye. Speak your goal aloud as a verbal vision and then document the vision of your goal on paper or your computer. Make a personal

Understanding The Importance of Goals

commitment to your Self to document your goals in the form of the Measurable Action Plan presented in this chapter. And resolve to follow your Measurable Action Plan no matter what obstacles life places in your path. The benefits and rewards from your efforts will change your life.

The Evaluation of Self Test

Quiz Three

Answer all of the questions on a sheet of paper or in your journal. Answer them to the best of your ability. And remember there are no wrong answers. What you write is for your benefit.

1. List two expectations that you now have after reading this chapter.
2. Name the three types of goals.
3. What is the purpose of having an objective for your goal?
4. What are the two main reasons the dreams and visions of most people go unfulfilled?
5. What does the acronym MAP stand for?
6. List three examples of how a goal can be measured.
7. Write at least one goal for each category of your life situation.
    a) Relationships (Family, Business, Personal)
    b) Financial
    c) Health
    d) Employment / Career
    e) Spiritual
    f) Education (Professional, Personal Growth)
    g) Recreation / Leisure

Understanding The Importance of Goals

Relax.

Smile.

Complete the prerequisite before continuing to the next chapter.

Chapter Six

Living a Balanced Life

Balance Defined

As you progress through this journey of change, you may get the feeling that something isn't quite right. You may not know what it is but it's there, causing a feeling of unease. Is it depression, anxiety, discontent, fear? Maybe. It could be one or all of these. Whatever it is, you can't quite put your finger on it or put a name to it.

What you may be feeling is simply an out of balance state. In this chapter, we will provide our definition of what balance is and provide Five Points on Balance to be mindful of. I don't think anyone can remain in a completely balanced state all of the time. But by being aware of these five points, you will be in a better position to identify when you are not in a state of balance and increase your ability to return to and remain in the best balanced state that is right for you.

Think for a minute... what does being in a state of balance mean to you? How would you define or describe it? Is it simply a feeling, when you feel good about your Self and everything happening in your life? Is it when you are at your peak performance in all situational categories? Is it when you are in rhythm with everything around you?

Or is it when you seem to be running on autopilot, with minimal thought given or needed in all situations? It would

Living a Balanced Life

be as if you are in a dance with life and you are leading while expending minimal effort. You're not thinking about living, you *are* living, present and mindful in each moment of your life.

Likewise, how would you define or describe what it is to be out of balance? Is it simply a feeling you have where you might topple over or fall uncontrollably? Is it when you get that need for a vacation from work or to get away from it all? Or is it similar to what I described earlier, a feeling of unease, depression, anxiety, discontent or fear. Could it be when you worry or think too much about what happened in the past or will happen in the future?

Your definition may include all of these, more, or none at all. But I think we all have some common examples of what it feels like to be in an out of a balanced state. I have found that one of the easiest ways to determine your state of balance is to determine your level of peace — specifically, peace of mind.

Peace of mind is the result of having a life in balance. A large part of your peace of mind is based on how you feel, how you feel about your Self as well as your life situations. When your mind is not at peace, it can affect every category of your life situations.

My definition of being in a perfect state of balance is described below.

It is when the peace that dwells within you permeates into every aspect of your being, internally as well as externally. When this peace is reflected in your mind, body, spirit, and emotions, when this peace creates life situations that are not problematic, your choices and decisions are in

The Evaluation of Self Test

alignment with your purpose and the focus of your attention is on the achievement of your goals.

There are countless other examples of what being in a state of balance is and how it can be determined and achieved. But for our purposes in this book, this is our definition and where we will focus our attention.

To start, there are two states of balance: you are either in balance or out of balance. There is no in-between. Next, your state of balance can be a result of internal influences or external influences. This can occur in four ways.

One, you can be internally balanced but externally out of balance. This means that you are at peace with your Self but outside of you, your life situations are problematic.

Two, you are out of balance internally and in balance externally. This is a state where your life situations are balanced but internally you may be overly conscious about every action you take which can make you moody and emotional about everything that occurs.

Three, you can be in a state where you are out of balance internally and externally which is the worst case scenario (no peace).

And four, the state we want to achieve and remain in, most of the time, is when you are both internally and externally balanced (peace).

A perfectly balanced state is hard to achieve, especially in today's world. The information age is having a great impact on our ability to remain at peace with ourselves and the world around us, especially when you consider the continuous stream of information that floods into our mind and influences us every day. And as our need or desire for this continuous stream of information builds within us, it can have the effect of keeping us in a state of imbalance without us even noticing its effect.

As I said in Chapter One, all of this information and the changes they bring "can leave us mentally fragmented, stressed, exhausted and fearful that our lives will change in an instant as a result of these ever changing times." But despite these and other influences, I want you to set a goal to achieve the state of balance we defined above.

The Five Points on Balance is being provided to help you achieve this state and to increase your ability to open the door to this peace whenever you like, as often as you like. We have already provided solutions to help you to achieve this state externally. This was provided in the PDS on Understanding your Life Situations in Chapter 2. In the next section, we will focus on the internal side of things.

The Five Points on Balance are focused on what happens inside of you — in your thoughts, in your body's reaction to these thoughts, the feelings and emotions that follow these thoughts, and finally the impact these thoughts have on your life situations.

The manner in which you express your feeling, emotions, and moods toward others says a lot about your state of balance. External volatility is a reflection of internal turmoil to some degree. The Five Points will focus on what's going on inside of you and provide some ideas on how to overcome the negative effects that these thoughts and feelings can have on your life.

The door to the peace that dwells within you can be opened by using just one of the five points. For some though, it may take all five. This will be determined by

The Evaluation of Self Test

how open and receptive you are to the ideas being provided. Everyone has this peace within them but the door to it may be locked. You must be willing to search for the key to unlock the door to your peace. Don't give up until you have applied every point in every combination to your unique situation. Finding the right key is part of your test.

The Five Points on Balance

Point One - Point of Reference

The peace that dwells within you is your Point of Reference. Your point of reference is your center. As you move away from this center, you move away from what can be considered your perfect state of balance. Your point of reference is what you return to when that feeling comes over you that cannot be defined. It is that feeling we called "being out of balance".

It is what you return to when your feelings, emotions, or moods take control of your thoughts and you begin to create problematic situations. This occurs mostly when you become dependent on external influences for your peace and happiness instead of your point of reference. You have to look within, internally, at this point of reference to return to center, to the center of your being where peace resides.

External influences come in many forms. We will categorize them as People (family, friends, coworkers, etc.), Places (employment location, a favorite leisure spot, living environment, etc.), and Things (money, a home, car, jewelry, clothing, etc.) to make them easier to identify. These three external influences have a tendency to move us away from our point of reference when we develop an attachment to them. We develop this attachment because they provide temporary peace. We find love in them, joy, stability, comfort, and happiness just knowing we have them in our lives or possession. But when they are removed, taken away or lost, an opposite effect can take control of our thoughts, emotions, feelings, and moods.

There is one thing you must always remember about external influences: they do not last forever and can disappear in an instant. And if your peace is attached to them, you can find your Self in a negative, unbalanced state for a lengthy period of time. You are basically setting your Self up for a roller coaster ride of negative thoughts, feelings, emotions, and moods. Because when these external influences are abruptly taken away — such as a special person, your favorite place to go, money, etc. — what do you have left? Just your Self.

But instead of looking internally to your point of reference for peace, happiness, comfort, and stability when the external influence is removed, you begin the search for the next something to find peace in again. And as a result, you will find that you will be continually searching for another external influence to fill the void left by the old one.

For me, I find that it is better to remember that peace dwells within. That it is my point of reference and a state of being that I can return to at any time. In Chapter 3, I wrote that my purpose was "to exist as a being of happiness and peace." This state is always available to me. It is the basis of my philosophy. And it is what keeps my thoughts, feelings, emotions, and moods from being influenced or

The Evaluation of Self Test

controlled by the world around me. It allows me to let go of external influences and attachments without having a negative impact on my state of being.

This point of reference, this peace, is in everyone. It cannot be taken from you and is always within reach. But it is unique to each individual. What can be considered a perfect state for me may not be the same for anyone else. You simply have to uncover it within your Self, under all the external influences and attachments and return to it whenever you feel your balance is sliding away from center.

So starting today, take a vow of celibacy — celibacy from a need for external influences to bring you peace, happiness, joy, comfort or stability. This will help you stay grounded even in an abundance of people, places, or things. Remember, they can all be taken away but your point of reference, your internal peace, will always remain in their absence.

Point Two - The Four Corners

As we live our lives day to day, one of our primary goals is to figure ourselves out. That is, to become aware of why we think and feel certain ways in certain situations. By doing so, it will bring us closer to or in contact with our point of reference. We can then be at peace with ourselves and the life we are living.

This goal is built into everyone even though some of us are not as mindful of it as others. This is an important goal that some of us never achieve. But people, like you, look for ways to achieve it.

Living a Balanced Life

One way to achieve it is to have a balanced approach to the four corners of your internal Self. The four corners of your internal Self are the Mental, Physical, Emotional, and Spiritual corners. Take a second or two to visualize a flat, square board balanced perfectly on a single point. The single point is, of course, your point of reference, your peace.

Each corner is interconnected and each corner is as equally important as the other in maintaining a perfect state of balance. If any one, two, or three of the corners are given an excessive amount of activity and awareness over an extended period of time, it will reduce the amount of activity and awareness that is available to the remaining corner(s). This can cause an out-of-balance state.

When any one or combination of the corners becomes too far out of balance with the others, the square board or rather your internal Self will eventually slide off its center, your point of reference. Each corner must be continually monitored to ensure an appropriate amount of activity and awareness is provided to them to maintain an overall state of balance.

The key to remember is to dedicate a fairly even amount of activity and awareness to each of the four corners. By doing so, it will help you to maintain balance on your point of reference as you live a life with purpose while pursuing your goals.

It will be easier for you to maintain balance on your point of reference by having a balanced approach to your Mental, Physical, Emotional, and Spiritual corners. There are countless ways to approach them by using different combinations of corners with varying amounts of activity

The Evaluation of Self Test

and awareness. Your goal is to find the combination that works best for you.

There are a few aspects of each corner that you should be mindful of when deciding on your approach. A brief description of each corner is being provided to help you build an understanding of some of the target areas that should be given the most activity and awareness.

These descriptions do not encompass everything that could be listed or that you can do. Include any additional target areas in your approach that are important and relevant to your unique life situation.

The Mental Corner

The Mental corner is your mind in action. The mind must be kept active with new information, new information that stimulates the natural creativity of your mind, that stimulates new ideas about your Self and the lifestyle you are living. Your mental corner can become stagnant and get caught up in a cycle of repetitive thoughts of the past if it is not provided the mental nourishment of new information.

This can lead to a reduction in your mental ability to create clear visual images for a purposeful, goal oriented future. The mental image that you have of your Self can also suffer as a result of this. Seek out different stimuli that affect your senses differently to create the types of situations you desire — situations that build Self-esteem and character so that you are continuously evolving into the person you want to be.

Feed your mind with new ideas by regularly reading or listening to idea-filled materials. These materials should

Living a Balanced Life

cover every category of your life situation and all matters of major importance. In addition, stay current with information related to your community, your chosen profession, world affairs, environmental issues, money, historical topics, and things that interest you.

Consider the information without judgment or necessarily believing all of it. Find the truth in it no matter how small to build an understanding of other points of view. Work toward being a more open minded person. Seek to understand and it will ultimately build your knowledge of your Self and the world around you.

Target areas for activity and awareness:

1. Read or listen to idea filled materials on a regular basis.
2. Stimulate your mind with different stimuli that stimulate all your senses.
3. Build an understanding of how your Self-image and subconscious mind can work for and against you.
4. Create visual images of the future you want to have.
5. **Stay** current with information related to each category of your life situation and all matters of major importance.
6. Work toward being more open minded to points of view that are different from your own. Find the differences interesting instead of a challenge to your own beliefs.

The Evaluation of Self Test

The Physical Corner

The Physical corner is your body in action. Your body allows you to physically accomplish your purpose and goals thus it must be maintained at its most optimum level of ability as long as possible as it ages over time. To accomplish this, you must take care of it. It must stay actively involved in physical activities until it no longer can. This requires eating and drinking in healthy moderation and being active on a daily basis.

The consumption of excessive amounts of food and drink without any or a minimum amount of physical activity is an unhealthy way to live. Over time, your body will tell the story of what you have or have not been doing.

Your body will display it externally with excessive weight and frequent injuries and internally with sickness, body aches, and disease. The pain from your unhealthy lifestyle will be most evident on your face and through the exhaustion or pain that you feel when you perform simple physical tasks.

Target areas for activity and awareness:

1. Schedule regular physical exams and wellness checks by certified physicians.
2. Provide your body with eight hours of sleep daily.
3. Eat healthy, nutritious and balanced meals daily and drink plenty of water.
4. Exercise your body as often as you can. Establish a fitness plan that you can follow that allows you to

engage in the activities you desire without encountering excessive levels of pain.
5. Maintain your weight at recommended levels for your age.
6. Discontinue the use of illegal drugs, abuse of prescription drugs, and cigarette smoking. Also, reduce or discontinue the consumption of alcoholic beverages.

Add any additional areas to the list that you may be struggling with. All of these areas can affect your ability to maintain balance. Learn your physical strengths as well as your limitations. Your body ages slowly as you get older without you even noticing it. Over time, mild pains and small injuries will begin to accumulate.

This is your body telling you to make an adjustment to your physical activities. In order to continue to do what you want to do physically when you want to do it, you must manage your physical body like everything else in your life.

Remember: you can participate in any physical activity you want to for most of your lifetime. It just will have to be done in healthy moderation.

The Spiritual Corner

The Spiritual corner is where your internal peace, faith, and compassion for others reside. It can be said it is where the source of life or the intelligence that directs life emanates. This corner can also hold different meanings for

The Evaluation of Self Test

different people because of the numerous amounts of faiths and religions that are practiced around the world.

In an effort to be open to varying points of view, here are four definitions from other sources that we can use as target areas for the Spiritual corner. Use them as well as your own beliefs to determine how you will approach this corner to keep it in balance with the others.

1. "the search for meaning in life events and a yearning for connectedness to the universe." (Coles 1990)

2. "a person's experience of, or a belief in, a power apart from his or her own existence." (Mohr 2006)

3. "a quality that goes beyond religious affiliation, that strives for inspiration, reverence, awe, meaning, and purpose, even in those who do not believe in God. The spiritual dimension tries to be in harmony with the universe, strives for answers about the infinite, and comes essentially into focus in times of emotional stress, physical (and mental) illness, loss, bereavement and death." (Murray and Zentner 1989:259)

4. ...refers to a broad set of principles that transcend all religions. Spirituality is about the relationship between ourselves and something larger. Spirituality means being in the right relationship with all that is. It is a stance of harmlessness toward all living beings and an understanding of their mutual interdependence." (Kaiser 2000)

For our purposes as related to your spiritual corner, it also includes how you practice your faith or religion in your church or community. Most popular religions teach the same philosophy of the spirit: treat others how you want to be treated. Our goal in this corner is to find the spirit of the oneness of all living spirits to practice this idea.

Whether it is chosen to be believed or not, we all come from the same source. We just come into the world from different vessels during different times, in different places, in different environments, surrounded by different people that think and behave in different ways. This is what makes each of us unique. But underneath our skin, we are all basically the same.

When we can all operate from this same idea of oneness, the world can move closer to a better state of balance. Because whether we like it or not, just as the four corners are connected, so are we.

I will leave the target areas for activity and awareness to your discretion based on your religious and or spiritual faith.

The Emotional Corner

The Emotional corner is primarily focused on how you "feel" at any given time and the moods you can fall into as a result of those feelings. It is about how you interact and behave with others when your emotions are at their highest and lowest points.

The Emotional corner can have a powerful influence over the other three if a certain amount of awareness and control isn't placed on it. Emotions can take over the mental corner with a flood of good or bad thoughts that direct the body to do good or bad things that can place the spirit in a good or bad state.

The Evaluation of Self Test

Controlling this corner can be a challenge for most people. They think they have little or no control over their emotions and their response to them. The key here is to become aware of your emotions as they arise and change how you respond to them as your awareness grows. You can start by answering the 5W1H questions when they arise — especially to negative emotions.

Questions like: "Why did I get so angry? Why am I so moody lately? Who am I allowing to continually get on my nerves and why? What is causing me to feel this way? How can I get control over these feelings of sadness? How can I change how I respond when this feeling arises?"

Build an understanding of the types of situations your emotions create in good moods and bad. And likewise, become aware of the types of situations that trigger your most unwanted emotions. Determine what types of stimuli you respond to in a negative manner as well as positive.

Use this information to gain control of your emotional corner. Use this information to control the types of situations you create or become involved in as a result of your emotions. Remember, feelings come and go continuously, along with the moods they produce. It is up to you to select the ones you respond to as well as how you respond.

Target areas for activity and awareness:

1. Determine what the positive emotions are that you would like to experience more of and work toward experiencing them more often.

Living a Balanced Life

2. Think about any negative emotional reactions you have to certain stimuli in certain situations and how your reactions can be changed for the better.
3. Examine your past behavior to determine how dominant your emotional corner is over the other three. Can it be more balanced?
4. Determine what your dominant negative emotions are and your level of control over them. Work toward gaining more control over them.
5. Explore whether or not your emotions are having a negative impact on how you interact and behave with other people. Especially in your personal relationships.
6. Practice the emotion of forgiveness as often as possible toward your Self and others.
7. Resolve issues by focusing more on facts and less emotion.

The Dark Corner

There is one more corner that should be touched on. This corner is kept in the dark for a lot of people. This corner is in a location that only you are aware of. The name of this corner is the Sexual corner. Sexuality has come "out of the closet" today more than ever but it still is a topic that can cause a lot of stress and anxiety. Science and technology have taken us to new levels in our ability to change our gender from one to the other and everywhere in between.

It has allowed many people to become who they feel they truly are inside. Numerous streams of media are

The Evaluation of Self Test

available now for all types of sexual education, exploration, and viewing. Still, there are some people that remain in the closet on the simplest aspects of their sexuality and cannot discuss the topic in open conversations.

The sexual corner is as important as the other four. This is because it affects all four corners unlike no other especially during our peak sexual years. I'm sure you have heard the phrase "sex drive." This corner can drive you to do all kinds of things, some of which are viewed a deviant and illegal.

A lot of deep dark secrets are kept in the sexual corner and there they should remain. Sexual pleasure that is viewed by most people and societies as pleasurable is one thing; illicit, unnatural desires are another.

The sexual corner can and does provide life with an added dimension that brings us love, children, peace, and happiness during our sexually active years. It affects all of our senses down to every nerve ending in our Mental, Physical, Spiritual, and Emotional corners.

A healthy sex life along with a healthy attitude towards your own sexuality as well as that of others promotes a state of balance in all corners of your internal Self. So give this corner the necessary amount of activity and awareness it needs to maintain balance with the four corners to maintain an optimum state of balance on your point of reference.

Living a Balanced Life

Target areas for activity and awareness:

1. Work through any inhibitions or problems you may be having related to sex or your sexuality.
2. Speak openly about your desires with whomever you are sexually involved with.
3. Take the necessary precautions to avoid any sexually transmitted diseases to protect your Self as well as the person you are involved with.
4. Get tested for HIV and other sexually transmitted diseases especially if your lifestyle warrants it.
5. Express your Self. Enjoy the many pleasures that this corner brings by exploring that which you desire without feelings of guilt, shame, or embarrassment.

A final point: when all the other corners and their target areas have been brought into balance and something still isn't quite right, look into the darkness of the Sexual corner for a solution. It may be something that needs to be brought into the light.

Point Three – Transitions

The third point on balance that you should be mindful of is transitions. A transition is a period of time where you change from one state of balance to another. They are caused by internal or external changes. Transitions that are caused by internal changes are those related to the Four Corners of Your Internal Self: the Mental, Physical, Emotional, Spiritual and also the Dark Corner. Transitions

The Evaluation of Self Test

that are caused by external changes are those related to each Category of your Life Situations: Relationships, Financial, Career/Employment, Health, Religion, and Recreation/Leisure.

A transition has only two directions of change and the direction that it moves at any given time is your choice:

1. It can move toward a state of balance or
2. It can move away from a state of balance

The period of time that a transition lasts is dependent upon how you adjust to the change that is occurring within your Self or your life situations. Moving away from balance for short periods of time is normal. Moving away from balance for long periods is not.

We all experience transitions but choose to handle them a bit differently. Your goal should be to extend the duration of a transition that moves you toward balance. And minimize the duration of a transition that moves you away from balance.

Part of your test is to 1) evaluate each corner of your internal Self and each category of your life situations to determine if you are in a transition and why. 2) What direction the majority of your transitions move in and why? 3) How long do you allow transitions that move you away from balance to last before you change direction and why? And then, 4) make any change that is necessary to ensure your Self and your life situations are moving toward balance most of the time if they are not.

Hopefully, as a result of what you have read in the previous chapters, your internal Self and external life situations are currently in a transition toward a more balanced state. Your thoughts, actions, and behavior should be focused on what you want, not what you don't want. You should be focused on your purpose and goals. You should be resolving problematic situations. If not, to this point, nothing you have read so far has helped you move toward a more balanced and peaceful life.

Change, for better or worse is usually uncomfortable. Whenever a change occurs in the way you think, feel, and view your life situations, you will naturally feel a bit unsettled and anxious. A state we earlier referred to as being in an out of balance state.

This is when you know you are in the midst of a transition. Your job is to identify the cause of it and change its direction if it is moving you away from balance. Sometimes it's obvious. But at other times it may take some conscious thought to determine the cause.

A good example of this is transitions that occur during intimate relationships, especially if you are married. These types of relationships can be in a state of change that moves toward and away from a state of balance continuously. All of the corners of your internal Self are involved as well as your life situations.

In the beginning, there is a period of friendship and infatuation that transitions to intimacy and love. This is when the relationship is moving toward a peaceful state of balance, most of the time. A few disagreements and misunderstandings may pop up but they are resolved quickly and easily.

Then there is the period when the relationship reaches a point where happiness and peace are experienced half the time and arguments, disagreements, and sadness take up the

The Evaluation of Self Test

other half. The relationship will tend to move toward and away from balance on a regular basis but there is enough peace to sustain it.

And unfortunately, some relationships transition away from balance and peace, most of the time. The relationship is filled with arguments, disagreements, and misunderstandings that are never really resolved. During these transitions, there are only a few periods when love, happiness, and peace are experienced in the same manner as when the relationship started.

You can easily lose your sense of balance with all of the internal and external changes an intimate relationship can produce. And the causes of the changes are never as obvious as they seem. They also have a tendency to build up a lot of negative energy and they usually end in an emotionally painful manner.

The time it takes to recover at the end of this type of relationship can last for weeks, months, or even years. The longer it takes, the longer the transition will last. Some people are never able to change the direction of this transition, at least for an extended period of time.

Remember everyone experiences transitions. Your interactions with people day to day will also cause transitions because of the influence that their imbalance can have on your state of being at any given time. It can happen suddenly, unexpectedly, and unknowingly like a sickness. It's almost as if they infect you with a contagious virus that affects every corner of your internal Self.

A simple interaction with another person or a frustrating situation can change your mood in an instant, if you allow it. Or it could be a long, slow line at the grocery

Living a Balanced Life

store, a call from a creditor, being caught in a storm without an umbrella, or a disagreement with a coworker or loved one. Even a short, calm, relaxed conversation with someone or a frown on someone's face can suddenly trigger a negative response from your senses that pulls you away from a good state of balance in a matter of seconds.

For example, you are in a good state of balance, moving toward a perfect state. You are at work and a coworker is upset. Due to the nature of the job, the two of you have to interact for the majority of the day. The coworker is continually complaining about the simplest of tasks and is speaking to you with an argumentative, unapologetic tone that gradually starts to annoy you.

You eventually lose your patience and control and give the person a piece of your mind. You are now clearly upset from the encounter and moving away from balance. The encounter continually enters your thoughts and your good day, good mood, and good state of balance have been shaken. The virus has just been passed to you and has thrown you into a transition away from balance.

Once you leave work you can let the events of the day pass through you. Or you can take the virus with you and pass it on to someone else because you are still carrying the unpleasantness of the day with you. This virus, this negative energy that was passed to you from a person that was in a transition away from balance can be more easily overcome when you become aware of the situation as it is occurring. This knowing allows you to respond with understanding in the moment.

This knowing enables you to answer most of the questions that will pop into your mind when the virus is

The Evaluation of Self Test

being passed such as: Why did he say that to me? Who does she think she is? What is their problem? Where do they think they're going with my ink pen? How did I get involved in this situation? They can't talk to me like that! Why did he cut in front of me like that?

This knowing allows you to see that you, as well as the other person, may be in the middle of a transition. Once the imbalance is recognized though, it can be prevented from spreading to anyone else. Now you have the opportunity to respond differently — in a more positive, understanding and compassionate manner.

Once the clouds of confusion have been cleared away, you can look for opportunities to resolve any known issues. You can then respond in a way that allows you to return to a better state of balance, and, allow another person experiencing a transition to possibly see the imbalance in themselves.

This awareness, this knowing can prevent countless disagreements and misunderstandings that often occur. It may also diffuse a situation that could escalate into one that becomes excessively problematic or even escalate into one that becomes violent.

One of the keys to a life of balance is to approach all situations with love, peace, and understanding. This approach should be your only motive when you address people especially during conflicts and problematic situations.

I once read a quote that said, "Life is about personal relationships between people and how we interact and behave with each other." When your interactions with others are in accordance with love, peace, and

Living a Balanced Life

understanding, you will always be able to maintain internal balance in most external situations.

Even when other people respond negatively as a result of their being in a transition, you can still choose to respond from a position of love, peace, and understanding. In doing so, you will spread a virus of a positive nature that becomes infectious and contagious enough to help other people change the direction of their own transition toward a more positive state of balance.

Without the help of others, a person can live the rest of their life in an unbalanced state. In normal cases though, as is the case in all transitions, a period of adjustment is required that each of us must go through to find balance again. We all need time to regain our focus and find some level of stability before we can move toward a better state of balance again.

Unfortunately, there will always be moments in your life when you experience powerfully negative people and problematic situations that place any peace you have in a shadow of fear, doubt, anxiety, depression, worry, etc. It will be hard not to transition away from a balanced state of peace in these types of situations.

But this is part of your test: Can you overcome the problems that change brings? Do you want to overcome them? Can you remain in a balanced state no matter who or what is pushing you off balance? It really is a choice. You must decide you will work toward improving your ability to resolve problems, disagreements, conflicts, and differences of opinion.

One way that will help you improve your skills in these areas will be to determine what type of person you are

The Evaluation of Self Test

when it comes to dealing with problems. Decide for your Self which statement best describes your relationship to problems.

1. I create problems most of the time.
2. I talk about problems most of the time.
3. I identify problems most of the time.
4. I ignore problems most of the time.
5. I identify and solve problems most of the time.

If your answer is not the fifth option, begin working on changing that behavior. Remember, change is hard so take it one day and one problem at a time until it becomes a natural instinct to sniff out a problem and resolve it. It may not be easy but just do your best in each situation as it arises.

There's an old saying that "misery loves company," so try to avoid being pulled into an argument by someone who is miserable. Strive to become a person that can identify a problem, discuss the issues calmly, rationally, and logically and then create solutions without clouding the conversation with negative emotions. Emotionally charged discussions rarely solve problems — on the contrary, they usually add more.

Problematic people and situations can infect you with a heavy amount of negative energy that must be countered with the positive energies of will power and determination. You must have the strength of will to push through until the situation changes to one that is more in line with your purpose and goals — to one that allows you to transition back toward a life in balance most of the time, all the time.

Living a Balanced Life

In closing, transitions are a natural response to change. It is not natural though for a transition to consume you and disrupt your state of balance for extended periods of time. If this has been a problem for you, set a goal to extend the duration of transitions that move you toward balance. And to minimize the duration of a transition that moves you away from balance.

As you bring more awareness of transitions to the forefront of your mind, you can minimize the discomfort of change, resolve problematic situations faster, and defend against the virus of imbalance in other people. This should promote an environment of love, peace, and understanding that will keep you moving toward a state of balance, most of the time, if not all.

Point Four - Self Induced Mental Obstacles

"The primary obstacles between you and your goals are usually mental. They are psychological and emotional in character; they are within your Self rather than in the situation around you." Brian Tracy, Goals Program

It is said that we can be our own worst enemy. This is clearly shown when we attempt to change our thoughts or behavior. As soon as we begin, a continuous dialogue of Self-defeating, Self-sabotaging, negative Self-talk from the voice in our head start up. Its only goal is to convince us that our attempts will fail. This negative Self-talk can block any of our attempts to move toward balance.

This dialogue is one of the primary reasons we don't succeed in our attempts to change our life situations, live

The Evaluation of Self Test

with purpose, or complete our goals. It is a sign that our mind is not at peace with our intentions. And as a result, we become an obstacle to our own good. We call these mental blocks that we alone create, Self-Induced Mental Obstacles.

A Self Induced Mental Obstacle is a thought or repetitious thought pattern that blocks movement toward balance. They are mental illusions of thought created by your imagination that affect every corner of your Self and your life situation. It is a struggle within your Self that begins when you try to change or attempt some great good for your Self.

Think for a minute: as you have progressed through these pages, how many times has a limiting belief crept in? What fearful thoughts have crept into your mind? Are you worried about how any of these proposed changes will affect you or someone's perception of you? What doubts do you have about being able to implement any of the Personal Development Solution's or pass the test?

If just one doubt about your ability to apply any of the concepts in this book to your life has repetitively entered your mind, you have been a victim of Self-Induced Mental Obstacles.

In his book, *Self-Discipline in 10 days*, Theodore Bryant refers to this inner conflict of one side wanting to do good (change) and the other side wanting to do bad (remain the same) as Dr. Jekyll and Mr. Hyde. Your negative Self-talk comes from Mr. Hyde.

Any time you try to complete a goal, Mr. Hyde begins his negative dialogue of, "Why are you doing this?" "This is a waste of time." "I'd rather be sitting by the pool or watching TV." "You're never going to finish any of these

Living a Balanced Life

goals so give up now." This negative Self-talk can go on and on and on until before you know it, you have ended all your attempts at achieving anything you set out to do.

This Self-defeating mental chatter goes straight to your subconscious. Your subconscious can help you achieve anything but it can also be your biggest enemy if it is constantly fed negative information. Some of Mr. Hyde's biggest weapons, as Bryant describes, that lurk in your subconscious are cynicism, defeatism, negativism, delayism, and escapism. I strongly recommend reading this captivating book on Self-discipline. It will help you overcome Mr. Hyde's weapons as well as the ones I describe below.

Our goal here is to help you be aware of some of the mental obstacles that can prevent you from moving toward balance. I will briefly describe three of the common obstacles you place in your own path with your negative Self-talk.

The first one is your Self. As stated earlier, we can be our own worst enemy. This becomes very evident when we evaluate ourselves. This book provides a means for you to evaluate and test your Self. It provides a means for you to bring awareness to your strengths and weaknesses so that you can bring balance and peace to your life. As you evaluate your Self you may find that hidden within your strengths, you have placed limits on your Self. Are you doing this? Are you being your own worst enemy by limiting your Self?

Or, do you know that you are limitless? That your ability to change is limitless? That each and every day is an opportunity to change if you choose to? That you are a

The Evaluation of Self Test

naturally creative being? And that your ability to create is limitless? Keep in mind though: you can create both good and bad. Are you creating obstacles or open pathways to success?

Unfortunately, a lot of us define and limit ourselves by our memories and experiences, especially the bad ones. They are usually the most hurtful, the most impactful to our lives. They are the ones that throw us out of balance faster than anything else. With repetition, they can lead us to believe, "This is who I am. This is me and this is all I can be."

But you are not just your memories and experiences. That's just what has happened in your life so far. You are limiting your Self, who you are or can be, if you continue to work within this imaginary boundary, this rigid thinking about what you can and cannot achieve.

In certain circumstances, limits are a good thing. Their benefits can be seen in almost every area of our lives. Some are put in place to protect us from injury to ourselves and others. For example alcohol/drug consumption, speed limits, age limits. Some are in place so we can leave some for others, i.e. limit of ten per customer when purchasing certain products. Limits are a necessary part of life. But the limits we place on ourselves when it comes to changing or improving our life situations are not.

Why do we place these limits on our Self? The reasons vary from person to person but they all start in our thinking. After beating your head against what you believe is a limit so many times, it's only natural that after a while you will give up. The negative thoughts can slowly pile up and begin to play like a song on a regular basis.

Living a Balanced Life

Such as: Why bother? You know you can't get past this. Why try? It will only get worse. No one will help. Just file for divorce, it will never work out. Why diet? You can never sustain it. Only certain people can do that and you're not one of them. You have never earned that much money so don't apply for that job. And the song can play on and on and on.

We have to stop focusing on and seeing every little flaw within our Self. Our vision, our image of ourselves in our mind's eye must change to overcome these mental obstacles. We must peel away all the layers of memories and experiences that have created our negative Self-talk. Once we accomplish this we can uncover the truth. And the truth is, we can push through any mental limit or obstacle we create once we change our mind and continuously apply the pressure of positive Self-talk on it.

In time, which will vary from person to person and situation to situation, the Self-induced obstacles you created and believe in can be overcome. So don't be discouraged if at first you don't succeed. Some layers of limited thinking are rigid and emotionally deeper than others. You have to try, try, and try again.

The second Self-Induced Mental Obstacle is Fear. Everyone experiences fear. Fear is a built-in, natural function that makes us aware of potentially life threatening situations. But when there are no life threatening situations for your fear mechanism to react to, it looks for other things. Things that are of a less threatening nature, physically, but can seem just as threatening mentally. When this occurs, your fearful thoughts can put your future

The Evaluation of Self Test

expectations or endeavors at risk of never being experienced.

Fear affects your balance because it is mentally heavy. And as a result, it can weigh just as heavily on all corners of your internal Self. It has a natural tendency to move you away from balance because it is the opposite of peace. You cannot be fearful and at peace at the same time.

This Self-defeating thought pattern can exhaust you mentally and cause you to lose any momentum or courage you may have built up toward the purposeful achievement of your goals. And as this thought pattern continues, before you know it, you will have placed a limit on what you think you can achieve. And that problematic life situation you wanted to change? It will continue, sometimes for years.

Without knowing it, you have sabotaged your Self and caused an internal corner or a life situation to begin the slide out of balance — to begin a slow transition away from peace. If this has happened to you, you have been a victim of the Self-Induced Mental Obstacle of Fear.

All Self Induced Mental Obstacles are the result of some form of fear-based thinking. Fear lies at the heart of questions like, "Will I like the change that change brings? Will the situation I'm changing be better or worse than the situation I'm now in? What if they laugh at me? What if they don't like me? What if I make a mistake? What will happen if I get divorced, lose weight, try a new field of employment, earn too much or too little money, move to another state or get married?

This type of fear based questioning about your future can go on and on until it dominates most of your thinking and causes many a sleepless night.

Living a Balanced Life

You have to decide how you want to live your life. You can choose to live in fear every day or live in freedom every day. So how would you rather live, in fear or freedom? Do you want to live in fear of the unknown, fear of failure, fear of embarrassment or shame? Or would you rather live free of fear? Free from the power of all mental obstacles that prevent you from achieving your purpose or goals and ultimately, prevent you from achieving a state of balance.

Read over the list below. Which of these fears apply to you? How and why?

1. Fear of Failure - Prevents us from doing the things that can move us forward to achieve our purpose and goals and ultimately find peace.
2. Fear of Rejection - We fear we are insufficient, lacking, demeaned, or diminished in some way because we were turned away or rejected.
3. Fear of Embarrassment - Public humiliation and judgment. You may be afraid that people will think badly of you or that you won't measure up in comparison to others.
4. Fear of Change - The unexpected or unknown creates tension, anxiety, and stress.
5. Fear of Pain - We try to avoid any type of Mental, Physical, Emotional, or Spiritual pain and any situations that can hurt us.

What other fears do you have? Which of your four corners does fear affect the most and why? What people or types of situations produce or trigger fear in you? What

The Evaluation of Self Test

Categories of your Life Situations does fear affect the most and why? What area(s) of your BEACH need to change to overcome your fears? How long does it take you to recover your balance after a fearful situation has passed? Are your fearful transition periods long or short most of the time? Your goal should be to eliminate or minimize the effect fear has on you in the future.

We all are afraid of something so first, accept that you have fear. Next, be courageous enough to look the source of your fear in the eye and act appropriately despite the fear. Even though the fear may still remain on a very subtle level, you will now know you have the courage to face your fear and prevent it from becoming an obstacle to the great expectations or endeavors you have planned for the future.

A final point: If fear becomes an obstacle that is so dominant that it becomes a phobia, seek professional help so that you can overcome it and enjoy all that the freedom from it provides.

And the third Self Induced Obstacle is Worry. Worry is the Weakness Of Repeatedly Reminding Your Self of something. It is the repetition of the same thought about the same situation. It can bring about an overwhelming rush of anxiety and stress about one or more life situations. When worry dominates your mind, it is an indicator that you are letting things happen instead of making things happen to your advantage.

It can start simply when your thoughts drift to "what if" questions. Questions like, "What if I fail the test? What if I don't get the job? What if the doctor says I need to have surgery? What if they discover I lied? What if I can't pay my bills? What if they don't like me? What if someone finds out what I did or didn't do?" And so on. Without knowing it, your guilty or doubtful conscience starts to brainstorm ways to get out of a situation, ways to cover it up or ways to avoid dealing with the situation altogether.

So what do you continually worry about? What aspects of your Self or your life situations do you worry about the most? What worries, about what, causes you to move away from balance most of the time? No matter what the source of your worrisome mind is, action must be taken to counter these repetitive thoughts. Without action, worry can turn into a Self-fulfilling prophecy.

Each time you create images of undesirable conclusions or expectations along with negative emotions about a situation, you increase the chances of it coming true. And unfortunately, the sources of our worries are based on things out of our control or assumptions we have made without knowing or checking the facts.

How do you counter a worrisome mind? Instead of allowing "what if" questions to dominate your thoughts, "act as if" the outcome of the situation that is the source of your worry will be favorable. Visualize or imagine positive outcomes that create positive expectations.

Focus on taking the action that is necessary to remove all or as much doubt as reasonably possible. Focus on preparing for any possible problematic outcomes or situations with a purposeful plan of action. Have plan A, B, and C ready so you can take immediate action to address any unfavorable outcomes.

Stop believing the lies you continually tell your Self or that others tell you. Stop the suffering YOU are creating for your Self. This repetitive, worried thinking is like mental

The Evaluation of Self Test

poison that you feed into your Self. Stop it! Stop reminding your Self of things that serve no purpose other than to cause worried thinking. Let it go! You are creating a mental obstacle that prevents you from moving toward a more balanced state.

Maintain a confident, optimistic frame of mind with regard to any anticipated situations. Focus your thoughts on the actions that need to be taken to take advantage of all of the options, opportunities, choices, and decisions that are available. You can then change the negative, repetitious thoughts of worry to the positive, inspirational thoughts of accomplishment, achievement, and success.

When the source of worry is cleared from your mind you can refocus your attention on your purpose and goals. You will not have to worry about future situations because you will be taking the action necessary in the present moment to ensure the best possible outcome.

And that's all we can expect of ourselves: to do our best, over and over until we achieve or receive what we want. And best of all, once your mind is free of worry, it can return to a more balanced, peaceful state.

Some other mental obstacles are:

- The thought of being in Trouble
- Allowing your Pride to get in the way of what you need to do

All mental obstacles have the same effect: they tend to move you away from balance.

Living a Balanced Life

Point Five - Finding the Way Back to Center

As I mentioned earlier, no one can remain in a state of balance all the time. There will always be occasions when we need to find our way back to center. When all of the other solutions and ideas presented in this chapter no longer serve you well, try some of these basic solutions to help you find your way back to center. Return to center using any method that works for you.

Love Your Self

First of all, you have to love your Self. You cannot have balance in your life if you don't love your Self. You have to love your Self enough to make whatever changes are necessary to bring balance back into your life. You have to make these changes for your Self regardless of what others think or what you think others think. Stop seeking or waiting on the approval of others to be who you want to be, to achieve what you want to achieve or go where you want to go.

Your life is based on your choices and decisions. But if you don't love your Self enough to take charge of your life, despite the disapproval of others or any perceived obstacles, then you deserve to be in the situation you are in — sliding away from center.

So acknowledge to your Self today that you love everything about you, who you were and who you are now, with all the flaws you commonly think of, because that person is you.

The Evaluation of Self Test

To start: have you looked at your Self lately? Looked at the person you think you are? If not, perform the following exercise.

Disrobe and stand naked and unashamed in front of a full length mirror. Look at your Self admiringly from head to toe and all around the edges. What emotions does your reflection produce? This is the external you that everyone sees and makes judgments about. Your body may have changed dramatically since you were younger especially if you are getting up in years.

As you gaze upon your body, think about the physical image you have created, strictly from a visual perspective. Is it a work of art? Is it an image you admire and are proud of? Or are you ashamed of the image you have created? And if so, why? And what are you doing about it?

Once you have an answer to these questions, ask your Self, "Do I love the image of my Self that I am presenting to the world? And remember, this is just an external image of who you are, not the internal you. Or is it? Is this external image a true reflection of who you are internally? Are the two aligned or completely different? Why? Dig deep for clues and answers.

This external portrait of your physical image can tell you a lot about your internal Self as in the Portrait of Dorian Gray I mentioned in Chapter 1. Do you love the person you see externally? Do you love the person internally that is creating the external image? This internal-external love needs to be in balance. You must love your Self completely, as a whole. Once you can acknowledge that you love your Self inside and out, you can begin

Living a Balanced Life

making the changes necessary to increase that love internally as well as externally.

Think about the questions listed above over until you have a clear perspective of who you are internally and externally. Accept that this is who you are now but not who you have to be moving forward. Now, close your eyes and speak to your Self aloud or silently. Say whatever is needed to establish that you love your Self, inside and out. It can be as simple as "I love the person I am and the person I am becoming," a favorite prayer, or anything else.

Repeat it until you believe it, until you feel it in the nerve endings of your body. Get inspired about this love for your Self. There should be nothing else in this world that you love more. This enthusiasm should spill over into every corner of your internal Self and be evident on your face.

Now, open your eyes and look at the physical image of the body that you reside in and state the same thing. Repeat it over and over as you look at your body lovingly in the mirror. This exhibits external love. And if you are looking in the mirror and you see something you don't like or if there is something internally that you don't like, get busy doing something to change it. You can then love who you are and the person you are becoming.

Perform this exercise as often as necessary to move toward balance as a whole: internally and externally. And perform this exercise as often as necessary to remain balanced once you achieve it. Because you really can't achieve a balanced life or love the life you are living if you don't really love the living creation that you are, inside and out.

The Evaluation of Self Test

RELAX

In some cases, all that you need to do to return to center is relax. Relax your mind and body to regain your balance and peace of mind. Simple relaxation techniques can reduce the stress and tension that can build up within you over time.

Usually, you don't even realize this built-up tension has even occurred. A simple sign is when you get irritable and overreact in situations you would normally handle with ease. This is a warning sign that people often ignore or don't give their full attention to. But whatever the situation, use some of these ideas to bring balance back into your life and move back to center.

<u>Renew</u> and refresh your Self by taking a hot bath or a nap when time permits. Pampering your Self and resting even in short periods can go a long way in allowing you to stop or slow the slide away from center. As an added bonus, the voice in your head may tell you what the cause and solution are to your balance issue during these periods of relaxation.

<u>Expand</u> your body and mind. Family and work are two of the dominant categories of life that we focus most of our attention on. This can create limited, constricted thinking. This is an indicator that you may need to expand your mind by reading something new to expand what you think about daily. Television works well for this but it can also cause the same problem when you get caught up in a routine of watching the same programs and commercials every day,

Living a Balanced Life

every week, at the same time in the same place in your home.

Expand your mind by feeding it some new information. Buy a book to read, listen to an audio program, or find a new website containing something refreshing to read about. In addition, expand your body in areas other than your stomach, specifically, your lungs. Perform activities that encourage deep breathing such as aerobic exercise, yoga, stretching/physical therapy movements or Tai Chi.

These activities encourage deep breathing, focused attention, and specific body movements that allow you to bring awareness into your body and mind. Do some research and find an activity that works best for you. The benefits will amaze you and move you back to center when you need it the most.

<u>Listen.</u> Sometimes we preoccupy ourselves with our Self and never listen to what's going on around us. When you find your Self moving away from center, you may need to start listening more to others. Take the time to really listen to what people are saying to understand what they are experiencing during their life journey. They may have a life experience or life situation that provides a solution that may be of some benefit to you.

Also, listen to your body and your mental Self-talk. What are you continually thinking about? What is your intuition telling you that you are ignoring? Listen to life around you. Listen to the birds, the rain, traffic, street noise, etc. Just listen to change your focus of attention for a few moments. You are sure to hear something that you have never noticed or heard before. But in order to do this

The Evaluation of Self Test

you have to pause for a moment; stop what you are doing and LISTEN.

Listen well and communicate with others as best you can. Stay open and don't stonewall; don't shut down. Better listening skills lead to better communication skills. Express your thoughts, feelings, and emotions as necessary to build positive energy that moves you toward balance or to remove negative energy that moves you away from balance.

<u>Allow</u> life to be as it is and work with it, in harmony with it. Work from a position of understanding. Try to be more understanding of your Self and others as you interact with different people in different places experiencing different things. This can also help other people return to their centers. Remember: you aren't the only person in the world that may need help returning to center.

Stop pushing, pulling, and struggling with what is and focus on what needs to be done. Some things are truly out of our control. You can't control everything. You can barely control your own actions. And everyone is dealing with this same internal struggle.

So look for the good in whatever you are struggling with. Approach situations with interest. Look for the solution and stop fighting against what is. The car is wrecked, now what? You lost your job, it's frustrating but now what?

Get past the emotional side of whatever the situation is and move on. At some point, you have to move on anyway. So don't waste too much energy trying to get over what is. As the saying goes, "it is what it is". So allow the situation

Living a Balanced Life

to be what it is, change what you can without struggling with it angrily. Because in the long run, nothing will really change until you change.

<u>X-ray</u> or ReXamine your Self. Often we are more critical of what other people are doing in their lives than we are of our own. Turn the x-ray machine on your own life to find out what is going on inside of you that is preventing you from returning to center. If you were a doctor, what would you prescribe to resolve the issue to move back toward center? Amongst all of these ideas, what is the best medication available to fix your unique situation?

Look at all of your symptoms. What would be your best recommendation if it was your mom, dad, or best friend who asked for your advice? Try it on your Self and see if it works. If not, you may need to look a little deeper. Perform the equivalent of an MRI or CT scan to get more clarity on what's really going on inside of you. Sometimes an x-ray just doesn't allow you to see into all aspects of your internal corners.

Balance is Completely Lost

And finally, seek help from others when you start feeling like balance has been completely lost. This can be help from family, friends, or professionals. There are counselors, therapists, and coaches that can assist you with your unique situation. You can also find plenty of help and encouragement in a place of worship or church. Sometimes, just fellowshipping with others can be enough to help move you back to center.

The Evaluation of Self Test

Also, volunteer work can provide just what you need to remind you that your situation is not as bad as you think it is. Hospitals, community groups, and charities are always looking for volunteers. You can gain a better appreciation for all that you have, internally as well as externally, when you get a firsthand look at some of the mental, physical, emotional, spiritual and yes, sexual situations other people are experiencing and overcoming.

Final Point – Exercise

Now that we have completed the five points on Balance, there is a final point I would like to provide to help achieve balance almost instantly. I often use this method when I get the feeling that I am losing balance. I came upon this meditation technique from watching the movie, *Eat, Pray, Love* with Julia Roberts. It was called Smile Meditation.

Answer these questions: How often do you smile? Why don't you smile more often? What prevents you from smiling more often? Do you smile all day, most of the day, sometimes or rarely? Be honest. Ask someone that you spend most of your day with to give you their opinion as a good point of reference. What's your answer? Your answer should be, at a minimum, most of the day. If not, try smile meditation to help change your frown into a smile.

I added one more step to the meditation technique: using an affirmation. You can choose to use the affirmation or just sit and smile as in the exercise we performed in chapter two. The affirmation is "I feel good and I feel good about it." That's it, "I feel good, and I feel good about it."

Living a Balanced Life

This one thought can bring everything back into balance. It affects all of the corners of your internal Self. It touches all of the senses. It can open you up mentally, physically, spiritually and emotionally to life, to just being, without dwelling upon all of the concerns that the world outside of you provides.

Here is the best way to use it. Start by putting a big smile on your face. Take two to three deep breaths to bring your Self into the moment. As you feel your Self starting to relax, take a deep breath and as you exhale, say to your Self aloud or in your mind, "I feel good." Take another deep breath and on the exhale say, "and I feel good about it." Deep breath, exhale, "I feel good." Deep breath, exhale, "and I feel good about it."

As you inhale, let your breath fill you up. Expand your Self. This is about you and no one else. This is Self-healing. Feel it from your head to your toes, throughout your body. Your smile should get bigger and bigger as the feeling of happiness fills your body and consumes your mind.

Each complete breath should build upon the next with energy, excitement, and the pure joy of just being. Bring as much emotion into it as you can until your smile is so intense it hurts your cheeks. Repeat the affirmation as many times as it takes until you reach the energy level and feeling of happiness you desire.

Feel good about your emotional state in that moment which should be passionate and powerful. Feel good about your spiritual state in that moment which should be at peace. Feel good about the feeling of aliveness that the breath you are taking is providing throughout your body.

The Evaluation of Self Test

And finally, feel good about the thought that you feel good — about the fact that you really feel good at that moment.

Relax into the fact that you are happy, content, and at peace. Don't bring anything about the past or the future into your mind. Just feel good and feel good about feeling good. This feeling can last as long as you allow it to last. This is the state you should want to be in all the time. This is a state of peace. This is a state of balance.

The following is a list of some of the benefits this approach can provide you with.

1. It puts a big, genuine smile on your face that can last as long as you want it to last.
2. It brings your awareness into the present moment.
3. It brings you into awareness of your breath.
4. It activates all of your sense perceptions.
5. It stimulates a heightened state of awareness of your surroundings.
6. It helps you to be more open and open minded with others.
7. It allows you to be engaged in any activity with a higher level of peace.
8. It helps you to feel good about any activity you are engaged in even if negative influences are present.

Perform this exercise at least once, with enthusiasm, to see the benefits it can provide you.

Balance Summary

During the writing of this chapter, I experienced a medical situation that related directly to the subject. While I

Living a Balanced Life

was out playing golf with a friend of mine, I started experiencing dizziness, loss of focus, and balance. This situation lasted the entire round. I came to find out the next day after a visit to the emergency room that I was experiencing vertigo.

For those of you that don't know, vertigo is a sensation of feeling off-balance. It's similar to the temporary dizzy spell you experience when you spin around in a circle too long. You might feel like you are spinning or that the world around you is spinning. The problem is normally related to your inner ear.

To resolve the problem the doctor provides you with dizziness medication and or performs what is called the Epley maneuver on you. This maneuver consists of having you lean back and in 30 to 60 second intervals rotating your head from left to right or vice versa. Simply put, you have to shake things up in your head in order to regain your balance.

It didn't work the first time for me. They tried it twice in the emergency room and I performed it on my Self several times at home. In addition, the Ear, Nose and Throat doctor I consulted provided me with some different moves to perform on a daily basis. Needless to say, it was frustrating and disappointing each time I performed the moves and the symptoms of vertigo continued.

But I had to continue these moves for well over a week until the symptoms passed. Vertigo caused me to lose my balance, my point of reference. I could feel all of my internal corners transition toward and away from center as each day passed. The obstacles of fear, doubt, and worry continually entered my mind. How long will this last? Am I

The Evaluation of Self Test

performing the moves correctly? Did I have a stroke? What if I never recover? Should I stop trying and give up?

I had to continually overcome these mental obstacles and continue the moves until I got better even though I couldn't see any positive results. It took me a while to realize I needed to relax. To have faith in what I was doing and continue the moves until the symptoms of vertigo ended.

You must do the same thing when you lose your balance. Situations will continually pop up in your life that that will make your head spin and throw you off balance. One or all of your corners will move away from center. You may find your Self transitioning toward and away from balance more than you like and Self-induced obstacles may flood your mind.

But you may need to do the same thing as I had to, shake things up in your head. Get control of your thoughts, what's inside of you, to gain your balance again. Roll things around in your mind, try some new things, brainstorm for new ideas or seek help from professionals like I did at the hospital. Or just simply relax.

Try one or all of the solutions that were provided in this chapter. Reread it. With each day that passes you may gain a new perspective on different aspects of your Self and the world around you. When you reread this chapter a few months or years from now, you may find different ways to apply this information that you hadn't thought about before.

Be creative. Don't give up too quickly just because you don't see any immediate results. They may be so minute that you don't even notice them. So stay disciplined and

Living a Balanced Life

persistent in your pursuit of the peace that dwells within you.

Remember: Everything is connected.

1. You bring balance into your life when the peace that dwells within you is reflected on your face, in your speech, your appearance, actions, and behavior.
2. You bring balance into your life when you know your point of reference.
3. You bring balance into your life when you ensure you are being fed in each corner of your internal Self, when you do not starve your Self or allow your Self to be starved by anyone or any institution, business, etc.
4. You bring balance into your life when you can challenge and push through the illusory wall of Self-induced mental obstacles.
5. You bring balance into your life when you are living with purpose, when your choices and decisions are in alignment with your purpose and your focus of attention is on the achievement of the goals you created as listed on your MAP.
6. You bring balance into your life when each category of your life situation is not in a problematic state.
7. You bring balance into your life when you see and hear the good in all things and situations.

The Evaluation of Self Test

Quiz Four

Answer all of the questions, to the best of your ability, on a sheet of paper or in your journal. Remember, there are no wrong answers. What you write is for your benefit.

1. Which corner of your internal Self is the most problematic?
2. Which corner do you lose balance in most of the time?
3. Which corner is the easiest to remain balanced in?
4. What target areas in which corner(s) need the most attention?
5. Which type of transition are you in most of the time?
6. What situations are the hardest for you to transition back to balance from?
7. Do your transitions last too long and why?
8. How long should you allow your Self to be in a transition that is moving you away from balance?
9. What will be the technique you use to break out of a negative transition?
10. What limits do you typically place on your Self and why?
11. What is the biggest limit you must overcome?
12. What is your biggest fear and why? How will you overcome it?

Living a Balanced Life

Relax.

Smile.

Complete the prerequisite before continuing to the next chapter.

Chapter Seven

The Review

Completion of Your Evaluation

Congratulations! You have completed your evaluation. Your evaluation was provided in the form of Personal Development Solutions. They served as your personal development tool to perform an evaluation of your Self. They provided you with a means to evaluate the purpose for your existence, your level of understanding regarding your life situations, your knowledge of setting goals, and finally, to evaluate if you are living a balanced life.

The evaluation provided you with numerous thought-provoking questions and ideas. Each solution provided information that should have opened a few doors in your mind and imagination. Additionally, it opened the doors to personal awareness, awareness of who you are as a being in this universe, awareness of the situations you have created or involved in, and awareness of the fact that you are participating in this journey through life with every other human being in this world.

You and everyone else are trying to accomplish the same thing: to live a fulfilling life of peace, happiness, and joy. But not everyone agrees on how this can be accomplished. This is what makes each one of us unique. Based on this premise, each person that reads this book will gain different insights into their Self and their life. And as a

The Review

result of this personal evaluation, each person will make different choices and decisions moving forward.

But in order to get the most out of this evaluation of your Self, you had to read all of the solutions, answer all of the questions that were presented, answer all of the quiz questions and complete all of the exercises. This was your test. It was a test to see if you would do the work that was necessary to complete a thorough evaluation of your Self by sitting down and writing answers to everything that was presented to you.

You were also challenged twice. You were asked to initial your name to acknowledge that you were ready to "make a choice to change" and that you "believed" you could change. By completing all of these requirements, you should have painted a pretty good picture of your Self in the form of your evaluation and at the same time, passed the test.

The Test

Your written answers to the questions presented to you during your evaluation were used to determine if you passed the test. They are the substance of your evaluation. Within these answers lies the information you need to change anything about your Self or your life. It required that you completed everything I mentioned earlier. Did you complete these requirements? Let's find out.

To have passed the test, at a minimum, you should now have in hand:

The Evaluation of Self Test

1. A purpose statement
2. A categorized list of your life situations
3. Your most problematic life situation
4. A top ten list of each area of your BEACH
5. Matters of major importance related to your BEACH
6. A philosophy with at least ten principles
7. A MAP with at least one major goal
8. Your most limiting Self-Induced Mental Obstacle
9. The one belief, environment, action, conditioned response and habit that, if you change it today, will have the greatest impact on your Self and life immediately?'
10. Answers to all of the quizzes
11. Completion of all exercises

If you have this information, you passed the test. You took advantage of everything that was presented and hopefully, you will use it to make changes that will benefit you in the days ahead. You took advantage of the opportunity to explore areas of your Self you may never have even considered or thought about in a while. Give your Self an A+.

If you only did some of the requirements, then you did your Self a disservice. You didn't take advantage of the opportunity provided by this book. You made a choice and decision to fall back into a comfort zone of complacency. You may have felt completing all the requirements were too hard or boring. But if you gave the material some consideration and came to the conclusion that it didn't apply to your unique situation, our goal was accomplished.

The Review

You at least gave the material some thought. Give your Self a C.

For those that completed less than half of the requirements, you didn't fail but you also didn't pass the test. You left your portrait unfinished. Did you even pick up the paintbrush? Now you need to look in the mirror and ask your Self, why? Why didn't't you take advantage of the opportunity you had to make some fresh choices and decisions about your life? Why were you lazy? Why did you procrastinate? Do you really want to change?

You have come this far to find out you are really still procrastinating at making a decision to really commit to changing your Self or your life situations for the better. You did not manage this situation very well.

You should begin again. You must start over and really do the work this time. If you choose not to, my only hope is that you found something within these pages that made you pause for a moment or two to reflect on an aspect of your Self or a life situation that you can change for the better when you are truly ready.

Summary

You have completed your evaluation and hopefully passed the test by doing the work. Even if you didn't complete all the work, the result of this evaluation and test is a win, win situation if you have read the entire book to this point. You have a wealth of information about your Self the your life situations available to you. What are you going to do with it? The decision is yours to make.

The Evaluation of Self Test

You may choose to continue on the same path you were on prior to reading this book. I am hopeful though that you will take immediate action. To succeed we must "keep hope alive". Hope is Having Our Purpose Envisioned. And it must remain envisioned as we move toward it step by step, day by day, and year by year. Hope can provide the encouragement we need to remain engaged in the process of change to make our dreams a reality.

At the beginning of this book, I talked about the choices and decisions I made at an early age. Upon receiving my evaluation from my supervisor, I always took time for a period of reflection. I reviewed each area of my evaluation to determine if I was satisfied with my grade.

And if I wasn't, I set some goals to ensure I did what was necessary to warrant a higher grade during the next evaluation period. I did my best to ensure my evaluations improved every year, or at a minimum, didn't decline. This is what you need to do now.

Take some time to reflect on the results of your Self-evaluation. What can you do better? What other areas of your Self or your life can you improve that was not covered in the Personal Development Solutions? What other areas need more of your focused attention? What other obstacles, mind-made or manmade, are you allowing to limit your progress in some way?

As you reflect, focus on *being versus having*. Bring awareness into the important situations in your life. Allow the peace that dwells within you to permeate into all that you do. Use your MAP to assist you in tracking and completing your goals. Remain open to new ideas and ways of thinking. Explore new ways of being and living. Don't

The Review

allow your Self to dwell in the stagnation of old, repetitive thinking.

And when you are ready to perform another evaluation on your Self, follow this process.

1. Evaluate your Self using the Personal Development Solutions to determine a need for change.
2. Look for options and opportunities to make choices and decisions.
3. Ensure decisions fall in line with your purpose and philosophy.
4. Create goals and objectives to add to your MAP.
5. Establish progress review points of measurable actions until goal achievement.
6. Monitor and evaluate the changes your actions have caused and their effects.
7. Maintain awareness of your level of balance, the duration of transitions moving away from balance, and the impact of Self Induced Mental Obstacles.
8. Repeat the process.

And remember: Always be that which you are trying to become. Exist as the person you want to be now, today, this very minute. Don't wait to be happy — be happy. Don't wait to be rich — exist in all of the rich abundances that this world provides. Smile often. Express your joy openly. And remain mindful that as you get older you may need to reevaluate what it is that you desire again and again. Time brings change whether you like it or not. And this is why you should always conduct periodic evaluations on your Self.

Chapter Eight

Period of Reflection

I was watching an episode of Sex in the City one evening and two of the ladies, Carrie and Charlotte, were attending a motivational seminar. I don't remember the name of the speaker or if she was just a fictional character. The speaker had opened the floor for comments and questions and Charlotte decided to make a comment. She didn't think the affirmations that the speaker recommended in her book were working or would ever work.

The speaker responded that maybe she wasn't giving her all or putting her Self all the way out there. Charlotte said that she was and she felt she would never find love again after her last relationship had ended. The speaker again said maybe she wasn't really putting her Self out there and not really giving her all.

Finally, Charlotte sat down feeling defeated and stated to Carrie that maybe the speaker was right. But then Carrie grabbed the microphone and said fiercely and defiantly to the speaker that her friend was really, really putting her Self out there.

The speaker, sticking to her guns and point said again, maybe she was holding back. In the final defiance of the speaker, her book and all her affirmations and motivational theories, Carrie said, "No, she is all the way out there." She

Period of Reflection

then held Charlotte's hand as a true act of friendship and support of her friend and what she had been dealing with.

I found this segment of the episode interesting because it seemed like the motivational speaker didn't want to admit that some people, as hard or as long as they may try, never see the results of positive thinking, affirmations, improved Self-discipline, or any other personal development solution that is available today. It seems as if this way of thinking or mindset may go against everything the speaker believes in or is "selling."

And the fact is, she can't. She knows that to bring about change in your Self and your life you must truly have an undying faith and belief that things will change. There can be no doubt.

But I also understand Carrie's point. For some people, even when they give their all and get all the way out there, they may not see the slightest improvement or change. The completion of your Self-evaluation, passing the test or reading, completing any other book, program, technique, etc. is not a guarantee you will be successful at achieving that which you desire.

You may give your all and get all the way out there and still not see any results. But if it is important enough to you, you will stay engaged in the process until you have that which you desire.

You must have faith. Faith causes us to act on what we haven't experienced yet, to believe in promises that haven't been fulfilled yet, and to have trust when our situations haven't changed yet. It could take more than a year or two before you see the results you want. Incremental change is

The Evaluation of Self Test

often hard to see. We can get so caught up in wanting it now that we lose patience with the process and give up.

But this is not for you. Because you now know that in order to start the change process, you must establish a purpose for your state of being, for your existence. You now know that you have to establish a philosophy to follow day to day that is in alignment with your purpose. You are aware that you must align your life situations with your philosophical principles of behavior to exist with purpose.

You now know that you must set goals to achieve the success you want and to continually resolve problematic situations. And you now know that if you allow the peace that dwells within you to permeate into your mental, physical, spiritual and emotional states of being, you will live with balance while existing as a purposeful creation of the creator, a purposeful creation of God.

Notes

About the Author

Anthony Vann resides in the city of Douglasville, Ga., 20 miles outside of Atlanta. He is a veteran of the United States Navy where he served his country for twenty one years.

He is an honor graduate of Saint Leo University where he obtained a Bachelor's Degree in Human Resource Management. He has held numerous positions in leadership and management in the Navy and corporate America. He has counseled, advised and evaluated hundreds of people during his lifetime.

Anthony welcomes any and all feedback regarding this creative work. Feel free to reach out and contact him at any time via the email address and social media links listed below.

Email: anthonyevann@att.net

Facebook: Anthony Vann
(Retired and Loving It)

Twitter: @anthonyevann1

Notes

Printed in Great Britain
by Amazon